THE WAY
PEOPLE
LIVE

Life in an Amish Community

Titles in The Way People Live series include:

THE WAY
PEOPLE
LIVE

Life in an Amish Community

by
Katherine Wagner

Lucent Books, P.O. Box 289011, San Diego, CA 92198-9011

To my mother, Doreen Jones Wagner

Library of Congress Cataloging-in-Publication Data

Wagner, Katherine, 1957–
    Life in an Amish community / by Katherine Wagner.
        p. cm. — (The way people live)
    Includes bibliographical references (p.   ) and index.
    ISBN 1-56006-654-7 (alk. paper)
    1. Amish—United States—Social life and customs—Juvenile literature.
[1. Amish.] I. Title. II. Series.
    E184.M45 W34 2001
    973'.088'287—dc21

                                        00-013118

21.95

Contents

Discovering the Humanity in Us All

Books in The Way People Live series focus on groups of people in a wide variety of circumstances, settings, and time periods. Some books focus on different cultural groups, others on people in a particular historical time period, while others cover people involved in a specific event. Each book emphasizes the daily routines, personal and historical struggles, and achievements of people from all walks of life.

To really understand any culture, it is necessary to strip the mind of the common notions we hold about groups of people. These stereotypes are the archenemies of learning. It does not even matter whether the stereotypes are positive or negative; they are confining and tight. Removing them is a challenge that's not easily met, as anyone who has ever tried it will admit. Ideas that do not fit into the templates we create are unwelcome visitors—ones we would prefer remain quietly in a corner or forgotten room.

The cowboy of the Old West is a good example of such confining roles. The cowboy was courageous, yet soft-spoken. His time (it is always a he, in our template) was spent alternatively saving a rancher's daughter from certain death on a runaway stagecoach, or shooting it out with rustlers. At times, of course, he was likely to get a little crazy in town after a trail drive, but for the most part, he was the epitome of inner strength. It is disconcerting to find out that the cowboy is human, even a bit childish. Can it really be true that cowboys would line up to help the cook on the trail drive grind coffee, just hoping he would give them a little stick of peppermint candy that came with the coffee shipment? The idea of tough cowboys vying with one another to help "Coosie" (as they called their cooks) for a bit of candy seems silly and out of place.

So is the vision of Eskimos playing video games and watching MTV, living in prefab housing in the Arctic. It just does not fit with what "Eskimo" means. We are far more comfortable with snow igloos and whale blubber, harpoons and kayaks.

Although the cultures dealt with in Lucent's The Way People Live series are often historically and socially well known, the emphasis is on the personal aspects of life. Groups of people, while unquestionably affected by their politics and their governmental structures, are more than those institutions. How do people in a particular time and place educate their children? What do they eat? And how do they build their houses? What kinds of work do they do? What kinds of games do they enjoy? The answers to these questions bring these cultures to life. People's lives are revealed in the particulars, and only by knowing the particulars can we understand these cultures' will to survive and their moments of weakness and greatness.

This is not to say that understanding politics does not help to understand a culture. There is no question that the Warsaw ghetto, for example, was a culture that was brought about by the politics and social ideas of Adolf

Hitler and the Third Reich. But the Jews who were crowded together in the ghetto cannot be understood by the Reich's politics. Their life was a day-to-day battle for existence, and the creativity and methods they used to prolong their lives is a vital story of human perseverance that would be denied by focusing only on the institutions of Hitler's Germany. Knowing that children as young as five or six outwitted Nazi guards on a daily basis, that Jewish policemen helped the Germans control the ghetto, that children attended secret schools in the ghetto and even earned diplomas—these are the things that reveal the fabric of life, that can inspire, intrigue, and amaze.

Books in The Way People Live series allow both the casual reader and the student to see humans as victims, heroes, and onlookers. And although humans act in ways that can fill us with feelings of sorrow and revulsion, it is important to remember that "hero," "predator," and "victim" are dangerous terms. Heaping undue pity or praise on people reduces them to objects, and strips them of their humanity.

Seeing the Jews of Warsaw only as victims is to deny their humanity. Seeing them only as they appear in surviving photos, staring at the camera with infinite sadness, is limiting, both to them and to those who want to understand them. To an object of pity, the only appropriate response becomes "Those poor creatures!" and that reduces both the quality of their struggle and the depth of their despair. No one is served by such two-dimensional views of people and their cultures.

With this in mind, The Way People Live series strives to flesh out the traditional, two-dimensional views of people in various cultures and historical circumstances. Using a wide variety of primary quotations—the words not only of the politicians and government leaders, but of the real people whose lives are being examined—each book in the series attempts to show an honest and complete picture of a culture removed from our own by time or space.

By examining cultures in this way, the reader will notice not only the glaring differences from his or her own culture, but also will be struck by the similarities. For indeed, people share common needs—warmth, good company, stability, and affirmation from others. Ultimately, seeing how people really live, or have lived, can only enrich our understanding of ourselves.

An Inherited Way of Life

The Amish are a peaceful, agricultural, religious society of people who believe in a life of discipline and hard work. Affiliation with the Amish church isn't just a matter of attending services on Sunday. The Amish live by the tenets of their faith twenty-four hours a day, seven days a week. While ceremonies and rituals are important to the Amish, their religious beliefs go beyond these observances and extend into day-to-day activities. They belong to close-knit communities organized around long-established customs and traditions to which members must adhere. To be Amish means attending church services. But it also means choosing to plow a field with a horse, hang the laundry to dry in the breeze, and learn lessons in a one-room schoolhouse.

Many of the outward signs, or symbols, that people associate with the Amish—such as plain clothes or the horse and buggy—date back hundreds of years. In a world where new is generally considered better, a culture that embraces the old and familiar seems odd. For this reason, outsiders often find it difficult to understand why the Amish dress and live the way they do. In the magazine *Family Life*, an Amish writer explains his reasons for continuing to follow a traditional lifestyle: "For myself, I prefer to go by the collective decisions that have been made and handed down to us over many generations. Is there not a real danger that if we throw out what we have inherited from our forebears, we may be missing something we will not be able to replace?"[1]

For hundreds of years, the Amish and their forebears, the Anabaptists, were deprived of basic rights, such as land ownership, in their native European homelands. After settling in North America in the 1700s, the Amish began establishing church communities. These rural settlements became safe havens where the Amish could practice their religion in peace.

The Sacred in Everyday Life

To the Amish, the sacred is reflected in all aspects of life. When Sue Bender, author of the book *Plain and Simple*, lived with several Amish families, she learned that even routine activities have a religious significance:

> As the days passed, I felt I was living in a still-life painting. In the background was a soft, sweeping farm landscape, and in the foreground were many people, all busy doing their chores with silent grace.
>
> Everything was a ritual.
>
> Doing the dishes, mowing the lawn, baking bread, quilting, canning, hanging out the laundry, picking fresh produce, weeding. Friday: housecleaning; Saturday: mowing the lawn; Monday: washing. . . . No distinction was made between the sacred and the everyday.
>
> Five minutes in the early morning and five minutes in the evening were devoted to prayer. The rest of the day was spent living

their beliefs. Their life was all one piece. It was all sacred—and all ordinary.[2]

Highly Regulated Society

The apparent simplicity of everyday Amish life can be misleading. Although it appears plain to outside observers, it reflects a society that is highly regulated. Members must adhere to established standards of behavior, dress, and speech. These standards can be confusing to outsiders, especially because many of the standards for Amish life seem contradictory. For example, although Amish community members cannot own or drive cars, they are allowed to ride in them and often hire drivers to take them long distances. To the Amish this is not a double standard. They cannot own a car themselves

An Amish farmer works his field using a horse-drawn plow.

because car ownership might make community members more mobile and cause the breakdown of the family groups that are so important to the Amish. But just riding in a car, on a limited basis, they contend, will most likely not keep members away from their families for very long.

For these reasons, Amish society is like an onion, which, when peeled, exposes hidden layers. To understand the Amish, it is necessary to understand their reasons for living as they do. At the heart of that understanding are the standards of conduct that community members follow.

CHAPTER 1 "A Sacred Trust"

The Amish are an Old World society living in a modern, fast-paced world. They don't readily embrace new technology. Instead, they prefer to follow time-tested customs and traditions. By honoring these values, the Amish have created a unique cultural heritage that serves as a testament to their faith. As one Amishman said, "Tradition to us is a sacred trust, and it is part of our religion to uphold and adhere to the ideals of our forefathers."[3]

Follow the Rules

The set of rules and regulations that govern everyday life in an Amish community is known as the *Ordnung* (pronounced Ott-ning). The *Ordnung* has been passed down from one generation to the next and exists in two forms. The first part, which is printed, dates from the beginning of the Amish church in the late 1500s. It includes the regulations that church leaders adopted at special conferences held during the church's early years. This part of the *Ordnung* provides the basic tenets, or foundation, of the church. All Amish communities adhere to these basic principles, which include living apart from the rest of society, not participating in wars, and shunning or avoiding members who do not follow the rules.

The second part of the *Ordnung* is unwritten and offers guidelines on how to apply fundamental tenets to modern-day situations. This part of the *Ordnung* varies from one church district to another, but all members in a given district know the rules for their community. As a whole, the *Ordnung* provides the rules for living. Community members demonstrate the *Ordnung* in the way they dress and behave. Children learn the specific rules and regulations for their district by interacting with and observing elders in the community.

Although the *Ordnung* differs in detail among districts, common restrictions and

Amish children learn the rules of the Ordnung *from their elders.*

requirements are strictly observed. Most districts limit the use or ownership of telephones, electricity, and central heating systems, for example. Typically, the *Ordnung* requires members to wear plain clothes, not attend school past the eighth grade, and use a German dialect known as Pennsylvania Dutch when speaking with other community members. Violating the *Ordnung* is a very serious offense and members who do so face possible expulsion from the group.

The Brim of a Hat

Within their communities, the Amish maintain rigid standards of dress and behavior. By adhering to these standards, members show their willingness to obey the church's teachings. Sociologist John Hostetler, who was reared in an Amish community, relates a story from his youth that illustrates how these standards extend to the width of the brim of a man's hat. Among Amish groups, stricter congregations require men to wear hats with wider brims than men in more liberal groups. Thus, when Hostetler's family moved from Pennsylvania and joined a group in Iowa, the men in his family used scissors to cut some of the brim off their hats. Hostetler notes that this action "made my brother and me more acceptable to the new community of Amish."[4] Although an outsider might not notice such a subtle difference, to the Amish, this type of small detail is significant.

The width of a man's hat brim identifies the strictness of his congregation.

Members of Amish communities willingly sacrifice individual needs for the good of their group.

Separate from the World

Because everyone in a given district follows the same set of rules, there is a great deal of uniformity within the group. This uniformity gives members a strong sense of identity and more clearly distinguishes them from outsiders. This unique identity is important to the Amish because they believe biblical passages require them to remain separate from others and because they view the non-Amish world as sinful. Hostetler notes that the Amish classify groups "according to their shades of worldliness."[5] The Amish define worldliness as behavior or goods that are generally prohibited in most Amish communities, including cars, movies, television, and higher education. The Amish limit or restrict the amount of time they spend with members of groups that allow worldly behavior or goods. The Amish respect other people and cultures, however, and usually get along well with their non-Amish neighbors.

Demut Versus *Hochmut*

Uniformity within the group serves another purpose as well. It promotes humility, or *De-*mut in the Pennsylvania Dutch dialect, a highly valued trait. Humility is the opposite of pride, or *Hochmut*, a feeling the Amish do their best to avoid. Throughout their lives, Amish members are reminded of the importance of humility. As Donald B. Kraybill, an expert on Amish culture, writes, "The Amish believe that proud individuals tack their name on everything, draw attention to themselves, and take personal credit for everything. The humble individual, by contrast, freely gives time and effort to strengthen the community."[6]

Gelassenheit

One of the greatest strengths of the Amish community is the fact that members willingly sacrifice individual needs and wants for the good of the group. This behavior can be explained by the word *Gelassenheit* (gay-LAS-en-hite), which is difficult to translate but roughly means a willingness to yield to a higher authority. For a child, older siblings, parents, and teachers are all higher authorities. For adults, higher authorities include church leaders, God, and tradition. According to Kraybill, schoolchildren learn the motto JOY, which stands for "*Jesus* is first, *you* are last, and *others* are in between."[7] JOY is an example of *Gelassenheit* because it teaches children to put others before themselves.

Gelassenheit influences the way the Amish think, behave, and dress. Calmness, obedience, and humility are all part of *Gelassenheit*. Members learn to give up their individuality to promote group harmony, for as one Amish writer notes, "The goal of Amish life is a tame, gentle, and domesticated self, yielded to the community's larger goals."[8]

The Clothing of the Faithful

Simplicity in clothing styles is another example of *Gelassenheit*. Amish clothing styles don't reflect individual tastes or the latest fashion trends. Instead, community members wear distinctive, Old World–style clothes that resemble the peasant fashions of eighteenth-century Europe. Around 1900 the Amish stopped adopting new fashions and chose to maintain their traditional styles. Since then, Amish clothing has remained so consistent that the apparel of Amish teenagers today is

Amish clothes are simple, plain, and modest. This woman's bonnet, dress, and black cape cover her almost completely.

Hook and Eyers

The Amish earned the nickname *Häftler* (hook and eyers) because of their preference to use hook-and-eye closures instead of buttons as fasteners for clothing. Buttons are forbidden on certain items, such as men's vests, but allowed on others, including children's clothing. The ban on buttons goes back to the days of Jacob Ammann, the founder of the Amish sect. At that time, buttons were the fashion rage in Paris and a way to display wealth. *The Amish in Their Own Words*, edited by Brad Igou, includes a letter from an Amish writer who explains the ban on buttons: "Many church leaders in Jacob Ammann's time, no doubt, could not understand why any Christian would want to adorn himself with costly, flashy, and showy buttons. Especially when something as convenient and practical as hooks and eyes was readily available."

The writer goes on to explain that another Amish objection to buttons is their association with military uniforms. During the Middle Ages, the buttons on soldiers' shirts were switched from the left side to the right side. This change allowed the soldier to unbutton his coat more quickly to draw a sword. As devout pacifists, the Amish refuse to wear any fashions or symbols that relate to the military.

nearly identical to that of their grandparents or great-grandparents.

Amish clothes fit loosely and serve the standard of modesty. An adult woman's wardrobe includes a one-piece dress, cape, apron, dark stockings, and black lace-up boots. The cape covers the shoulders and chest and is important because, as one woman writes, "Without a cape, we make an unnecessary show of our figures."[9]

Tradition and custom dictate the variations in Amish women's dress. For instance, to attend church services she puts on a white cape and apron, but for everyday use, she wears a dress, cape, and apron that are all the same color. Women don't use zippers or buttons; instead they fasten their clothes with straight pins, snaps, hooks-and-eyes, or Velcro. During winter months, a woman wears a black shawl, which is folded either into a rectangle or triangle depending on the local custom.

The *Ordnung* also requires women to wear a covering called a prayer cap on their head at all times. Babies as young as six weeks old wear prayer caps. The prayer cap is usually white but in some districts, unmarried women wear black prayer caps to church service. Women spend considerable time ironing their prayer caps, which are made of a delicate organdy material and have many tiny pleats. Traditionally women have worn black bonnets outdoors, but in recent years an increasing number of women have stopped wearing them.

Children's clothing styles are similar to adult fashions. Young girls wear a one-piece dress with a full-length sleeveless apron over it. Sometimes a pocket is sewn into the front of the dress, covered by the apron. The apron is usually white for church services and the same color as the dress for everyday use. Clothes for children are fashioned with many pleats and tucks, which can be let out as the child grows in the service of practicality and long use. Also to that end, because Amish dress styles don't change, garments can be passed down to younger siblings.

Tradition and custom also determine the styles and types of clothes that men and boys wear. Perhaps the most recognizable feature of men's clothing is the wide-brimmed hat. Men and boys are required to wear a black felt or straw brimmed hat at all times outside. For

Amish women wear white organdy prayer caps all the time.

everyday situations, men and boys typically wear broadfall trousers (loose pants), suspenders, a white or pastel-colored shirt, and black shoes. For church services and special occasions, a man wears a frock coat and vest.

The *Ordnung* does not allow outside pockets or hip pockets. A pocket visible to others is forbidden because the wearer might put small items into it and this could lead to *Hochmut*. Likewise, jewelry is forbidden, including wedding rings, because the Amish wear only items that serve a useful purpose. One Amish writer explains that, although gold jewelry would be forbidden, "even gold may be worn if it is for some useful purpose, such as dentistry work." [10]

Touches of Color

The unique clothing demands of the Amish make shopping for and buying clothes in mainstream retail malls difficult. Although certain items, such as men's hats, are often purchased, women still sew most of their families' clothes, using homemade brown-paper patterns. Because the *Ordnung* forbids electricity, women use foot-operated treadle machines, which are placed near windows to take advantage of natural light.

Although Amish women sew clothes the old-fashioned way, they prefer to use modern fabrics, such as polyester, which are easy to wash and do not need to be ironed. Women generally buy cloth from a fabric store but, to save money, also reuse material from other sources to make clothing for their families. A physician who grew up Amish recalls that his mother made shirts and slips from white cotton feed bags used in the family's feed business. "She prepared the cotton material by washing and bleaching the bags a number of times," he explains. "This softened the material and disguised the lettering on the bags."[11]

Color is an integral part of Amish life. A common misconception by outsiders is that the Amish wear only black. Although black is a common color, as it is considered joyful by the Amish, members do wear other colors. Their clothes must be subdued and solid colored, however. Children's fashions are nearly identical to adult styles but include a broader range of color choices, including pastels. Writer Sue Bender went to live for several months with the Amish. Her first impression when she saw the Amish was that they "all looked alike. Alike and austere." Moments later, though, she had a change of heart. "When I looked again, I saw that their clothing wasn't all drab. Touches of bright purple, electric green, vibrant blue showed in their blouses and shirts. The intense color created a dramatic contrast in the midst of all the plainness."[12]

Plain Grooming

Simplicity and plainness go beyond clothing styles. Both standards also extend to personal grooming. Amish women don't follow the elaborate beauty routine of many non-Amish women. For instance, an Amish woman doesn't put on makeup, pluck her eyebrows, or shave her legs because, as Kraybill notes, these actions would be "tampering with God's creation."[13] Furthermore, women and girls never cut their hair, and wear it parted in the middle and pulled back into a bun.

Men's grooming styles are also regulated. An Amish man must wear a full, uncut beard, which he begins to grow after he is married. Mustaches are not allowed because they have been associated with the military in the past and the Amish are pacifists. Both boys and men wear their hair in a distinctive Amish style that resembles a bowl shape. The hair, which is combed straight down from the crown, reaches the collar except in the front where it is cut into bangs.

Married Amish men must grow beards but are not permitted to wear mustaches.

English as a Second Language

In outward appearance the Amish community differs markedly from the outside world. It also differs in its use of languages. The Amish are trilingual, meaning they speak three languages: Pennsylvania Dutch, English, and High German, or Hochdeutsch. The *Ordnung* regulates which language is to be spoken in a given social situation. Around the home or in the Amish community, for example, Pennsylvania Dutch, a German dialect, is spoken. (In this case, the word *Dutch* refers not to the Netherlands, but to the word *Deutsch*, meaning German.) This dialect is specifically an oral language spoken by groups of people whose ancestors arrived from Germany and settled primarily in southeastern Pennsylvania.

Pennsylvania Dutch has special significance to the Amish, as speaking in this dialect distances them from the *Englishers*, or non-Amish world. In the Amish magazine *Family Life*, a writer comments that just as it would be a loss not to know English, it would be wrong not to "pass on the German [Pennsylvania Dutch] to our children—that rich language our forebears left for us. . . . The value of that heritage is so great that we can't afford to lose it." [14]

In conversation with outsiders, though, the Amish switch to English. Furthermore, since Pennsylvania Dutch is a spoken language, the Amish also conduct all their written communication in English. Children learn the Pennsylvania Dutch dialect at home and in the community. They learn English at school, starting in the first grade.

Generally, the Amish don't have a pronounced accent when speaking English even though it's essentially a foreign language to them. In an excerpt from a letter in the *Blackboard Bulletin*, a newsletter for Amish teachers, one community member says:

I've often found that one problem we Amish have is in knowing how to pronounce English words. Many English words are not pronounced the way they look. There is also the problem of knowing where to put the accent. Part of the reason for this is because much of our contact with the outside world is reading rather than radio or television, so we don't hear words pronounced correctly. . . . Few people have the time to look up every word in the dictionary before pronouncing it! [15]

Schoolchildren also study High German, the language used at church services and in the Amish Bible. The name High German refers to the location of the language's origins, the mountainous region of Germany. The Amish never use this language for everyday conversation. In fact, most members know only enough to quote biblical passages, recite prayers, and sing hymns in German. Church leaders also must be able to preach in German, but even then they often throw in English and dialect words.

Horse Power

Just as the *Ordnung* regulates the clothes and language of the Amish, it also regulates their mode of travel. The Amish rely on horses as their main form of transportation and the horse has become a key symbol of the Amish faith. According to community members, Kraybill notes, using horses, instead of cars or tractors, is "tangible proof that [they] have not sold out to the glamour and glitter of high technology." [16]

Horse-powered transportation slows the pace of Amish life. A buggy can travel at speeds of only five to eight miles an hour. But getting somewhere quickly is not the point of Amish

The horse and buggy is standard transportation for Amish.

life, as writer Sue Bender learned during her stay with an Amish family. Of her first buggy ride, Bender says, "How restful the ride was, no rushing to pass another buggy or beat out a red light. . . . The hour it took to go five miles was slow enough to savor the landscape and still arrive on time."[17]

There are more than ninety types of buggies, and different styles serve different purposes. The most common is the standard enclosed carriage, which is the style most people associate with the Amish, although some Amish groups object to the enclosed buggy and use an open buggy instead. Young men of courting age use a single-seated, topless "bachelor" buggy, and farmers take their goods to town in a market wagon. A spring, or cab, wagon, serves as a pickup truck.

Though considerably less costly than a new car, a horse and buggy is still a major investment. Buggies, which are commonly made of oak, poplar, and hickory, can cost nearly five thousand dollars. A new buggy is treated with six or seven coats of paint and can last from fifteen to thirty years. Standardbred horses (retired racehorses) pull the buggies and range in price between six hundred and three thousand dollars.

Buggy Options

Depending on the rules of the particular community, a buggy might or might not be equipped with a dashboard, turn signals, windshield wipers, interior curtains, or hydraulic

Since retiring as a rural bus driver in Ohio, Jim Butterfield has used his car to transport Amish families to doctor appointments and to visit distant relatives. In this excerpt from his book *Driving the Amish*, Butterfield recalls a conversation with a farmer named Atlee, who hired Butterfield to drive him to a buggy maker.

The country roads were so quiet that we only saw one buggy and one other car the whole

ten miles back. That particular buggy had a kerosene lantern for light. The lantern frame held a round red glass at the back for a tail-light. That is what the most conservative branch of Amish use. Their buggies don't have storm fronts or even little windows in the side curtains.

"I like buggies and wagons," I said to Atlee. "But why do your people keep on using them instead of getting cars?"

He thought for a minute.

"We hold to the old ways. We like to do things like our ancestors did. We live close enough together so we can pretty much go where we wish with a horse. . . . I like going by horse and buggy . . . you actually see more from a buggy, and it's easier to stop and talk with someone. The horse-and-buggy pace helps to keep us together."

Amish people prefer the slower pace of the horse and buggy.

brakes. Even the color of the top of the buggy varies from area to area and groups can be distinguished by their "gray tops," "black tops," "yellow tops," or "white tops."

Despite safety features, slow-moving buggies can be a hazard on the roads. Over the years, there have been many accidents at night involving cars and buggies because automobile drivers are unable to see the unlit dark buggies. To prevent such accidents, the Amish put reflective tape and triangles on the backs of buggies to make them more visible. But some conservative Amish groups in Wisconsin and Minnesota have refused to use orange-red triangles. They say those warning signs are too bright and "worldly." Instead these groups use white reflective tape and hang a red lantern on the back.

The Amish travel primarily by nonmotorized means, but there are times when a horse and buggy is not practical. Although the Amish cannot own cars themselves, there are no restrictions on riding in cars. When church members have an appointment or want to visit someone who lives far away, they hire a car or van and driver. In this way, the Amish adhere to the rules of their community while taking advantage of new technology.

Some Amish use reflective triangles on the backs of their buggies to make them more visible to automobile traffic.

In the book *Amish Women*, writer Louise Stoltzfus gives an insider's view of how an Amish community considers changes to its *Ordnung*.

Members of the Amish church [do not] blindly submit to decisions made by the leaders without asking questions. Discussions about what new inventions, ideas, or habits should be permitted to enter community life are constant and involve everyone.

Women talk about them at quiltings and reunions. Men talk about them at barnraisings and haymakings. Husbands consult their wives. Preachers, often influenced by an abundance of freely stated opinions, get together and decide.

Once a decision is made, however, people are expected to conform. Those who decide not to conform or to leave will be confronted by church leaders.

The Decision to Change

The *Ordnung* is always evolving to reflect contemporary concerns and issues. For this reason, church districts regularly evaluate it and make changes as necessary. The Amish must constantly decide how much change their society can withstand. They will adopt new technology or loosen a restriction, but only if doing so does not put their culture at risk. "Each restriction we have is the result of some problem or misuse that the church faced at one time," notes an Amish writer. "When we face new problems, we must make decisions whether we want to act on them or not. When I was a boy, there was no rule against watching or owning a television set, for the simple reason that there was no television."[18] Amending the *Ordnung* is a democratic process. All baptized adult members of the community participate and have a voice in the matter.

"Where will this lead?"

In his book *Amish Society*, author John Hostetler tells how a Pennsylvania Amish district made the decision to allow members to own cars, something that had previously been banned. As a group, this Pennsylvania community decided that it was in their best interest to drop the restriction. In doing so, this group went against a long-standing Amish tradition not to use motorized vehicles.

Even before the issue of car ownership was raised, the Pennsylvania district had already modified its *Ordnung*. Though they still dressed in plain clothes, men in this district cut their hair shorter than was customary and farmers used tractors in the fields, two practices that more conservative groups do not permit. Despite having eased restrictions in the past, there was a great deal of debate about whether or not it was a good idea to allow car ownership. Several members had already been excommunicated from the church for buying cars and others were threatening to leave and join more progressive churches. Facing increasing pressure, the leaders of the congregation unanimously supported the change. From there, the issue was taken to the church assembly, where members voted overwhelmingly to adopt the new rule. Even so, one member, who had vetoed the resolution, noted her concerns when she said: "Where will this lead to, if our young people are given the privilege of going wherever they want?"[19]

The Amish uphold traditions that have been passed down to them through the years. The *Ordnung* provides guidance but is a living, and therefore evolving, code. The rules sometimes change, as they did in the community that voted to accept car ownership. Even so, the *Ordnung* is the law that guides Amish life and ties the community together.

A Community of Believers

The Amish live in small religious communities. Amish homes, which are interspersed with non-Amish, or *Englisher*, homes, dot America's rural landscape. In recent years the Amish population has been rapidly increasing, causing a strain on resources in older communities and leading young people to move and create new communities elsewhere. But every community, whether old or new, is organized in the same way and offers its members a place to worship, work, and socialize together.

Anabaptist Roots

It is impossible to understand the significance of community in Amish society without knowing the history of the church and its people. The sect originated in the 1500s with a group of religious reformers known as Anabaptists. The Anabaptists believed in adult (versus infant) baptism and strict separation of church and state. At the time, these concepts were extremely radical. Powerful church states ruled western Europe, and individuals who opposed these institutions faced harassment or death. The church states required infant baptisms, a rite the Anabaptists opposed on the grounds of their belief that joining a church should be a voluntary act. The group came to be called Anabaptists, meaning, "to be rebaptized," because most early members were baptized twice, once as infants and a second time as adults.

The Anabaptists paid dearly for their beliefs. Most were tortured and killed. The *Mar-*

The first Amish people were the Anabaptists, sixteenth-century religious reformers who were tortured and killed for their beliefs.

tyr's Mirror, a book written in 1610, records the ordeals of the Anabaptist martyrs and can be found in nearly every Amish home. The Amish remember and honor the sacrifices of these church founders. As one writer puts it: "We plain people often refer to our ancestors, the Anabaptists. Willingly, they offered up their lives and accepted death. Hardly a sermon is preached in our churches today without some mention being made of our forebears and what they suffered." [20]

Despite persecution, the Anabaptist movement grew. Eventually, government officials stopped killing the Anabaptists, but that did not mean that life was easy for them. Many people were imprisoned or forced to leave their homes. Members could not worship openly, so they often met in secret, at night, in woods or caves. And they did not keep any formal records.

Although the Anabaptists generally distrusted outsiders, they did have sympathetic friends and relatives, whom the Anabaptists called True-Hearted People. The Anabaptists were divided over whether or not they should accept help from these allies, however. Increasingly, a group of Anabaptists in the Alsace region of France and the Palatine region of Germany opposed associating with the True-Hearted People, whom they considered sinful. This group of Anabaptists first became the Swiss Mennonites and eventually became the Amish.

Jacob Ammann

In the mid-1500s, a former Catholic priest named Menno Simmons became a leader in the Dutch Anabaptist movement. So great was Simmons's influence that his followers became known as Mennonites. By the late 1600s, Mennonite groups existed in Holland and Switzerland.

The early trials of the Anabaptist martyrs were recorded in the book Martyr's Mirror.

In 1693, the Swiss Mennonite group underwent a split; at the forefront of this division was Jacob Ammann, a church elder, who advocated that the sacrament of Holy Communion should be held twice a year, instead of once, which was the Mennonite practice. He also wanted stricter enforcement of the practice of shunning, or social avoidance, of excommunicated members. Those who sided with Ammann were first called Amish Mennonite, and later simply Amish.

Although Ammann had a great influence on their religion, the Amish do not revere Ammann and actually know very little about him. In the book *Amish Society*, author John Hostetler quotes two Amishmen from 1830: "The birthplace of Jacob Aymen [Ammann] we have not ascertained, nor yet the exact place of residence—having never considered him a man of note, we do not deem the place of his nativity [birth] a matter of consequence." [21]

The Need to Move Westward

During the 1600s, local German and French nobles offered Swiss Mennonites, which included

The Amish practiced innovative agricultural techniques and proved themselves capable farmers.

the Amish, the opportunity to farm on land that had been devastated during the Thirty Years' War. The war, which lasted from 1618 to 1648, consisted of a series of European conflicts fought mainly in Germany. Although the Amish did not have extensive agricultural experience, they proved themselves capable farmers. They practiced innovative agricultural techniques such as feeding livestock indoors, rotating crops, and irrigating meadows. They also improved soil quality with animal fertilizers and the planting of

alfalfa and clover. Today the Amish continue to use these same farming techniques, which can transform dry land into sustainable fields.

The German rulers valued the contribution of the Amish, but failed to give the religion legal recognition. This meant that the Amish could not own land and pass their farms down to their children. In the 1700s, William Penn (1644–1718), an English Quaker who had been granted a charter in the New World by the king of England, invited oppressed religious groups throughout Europe to settle in his colony of Pennsylvania. Penn guaranteed the colonists they would have religious toleration and full participation in government if they joined, what he called, his "Holy Experiment." Although the Amish would have preferred to stay in their homelands, the promise of religious freedom led them to accept Penn's offer.

"A Voyage of 83 Days"

The first documented Amish immigrants to reach American shores arrived in October 1737 on the ship *Charming Nancy*. When the ship reached Philadelphia there were twenty-one Amish passengers onboard. Sailing across the Atlantic Ocean was not a pleasant experience. Food and water were scarce and usually contaminated. Disease was widespread. Many children died during the voyage. One observer noted that the people were "packed into the big boats as closely as herrings."[22] A fragment of the diary of Hans Jacob Kauffman, a passenger on the *Charming Nancy*, reads: "Landed in Philadelphia on the 18th and my wife and I left the ship on the 19th. A child was born to us on the 20th—died—wife recovered. A voyage of 83 days."[23]

The prospect of a perilous ocean crossing did not stop Amish immigration, however. During the 1700s, nearly five hundred Amish left Europe. Most Amish today can trace their ancestry to this small group of early colonists. In the 1800s, three thousand Amish settled in America.

These waves of Amish migration severely depleted the number of European members, and the small pockets of Amish who remained in the homelands were never able to form cohesive communities. They lost their unique identity and

The Eyes of a Hawk

To an Amish farmer, the concept of community encompasses much more than people. It also includes the animals, vegetation, terrain, and buildings in an area. In this excerpt from *Scratching the Woodchuck*, essayist David Kline recalls how seeing his neighborhood from a different perspective expanded his view of the small Amish community where he grew up. When Kline was twelve years old, a U.S. government official stopped at the Kline family farm.

When the young technician visited our farm he had a large aerial photograph of the entire neighborhood, which he spread out on the hood of his car. . . .

I looked at the map and marveled at the landscape from the air: the view the red-tailed hawk had when it soared high over the fields. There, meandering through the pasture field, was the creek where we fished and swam. And the woods with all its interesting creatures. There was the one-room schoolhouse with its massive white oak by the front entrance and the red oak next to the baseball backstop. I could already smell the freshly oiled wood floor and felt myself looking forward with anticipation to September when the new school year would begin. It was there on those three acres, after all, that the study of nature and creation and language and music and arithmetic and softball become one.

From that photograph my horizons broadened.

joined other churches, such as the Mennonites. As a result, there no longer are any Amish living in the countries where the sect began.

A New Life in America

The first Amish settlement, known as Northkill, was established in Berks County, Pennsylvania, in the 1730s. At its peak, it might have had 150 to 200 residents. According to a state historical marker, the settlement disbanded in 1757 when an Indian attack left a soldier and three members of one family dead. Another early settlement was Lancaster County, Pennsylvania. Today Lancaster County is the oldest existing settlement and the second largest in population. But in the 1700s, Lancaster, like most other settlements, consisted of small clusters of families whose primary concerns were little different than those of any other settlers. As one historian puts it, "The everyday life of Pennsylvania's Amish revolved around survival and producing an honest living as much as it did around Sunday worship service."[24]

Many Amish immigrants were poor farmers or millers with few resources to purchase land. A few, however, had amassed money before reaching America. These enterprising individuals bought large tracts of land when they arrived in the New World. They then subdivided and sold the land to family members and other Amish, who in turn subdivided and sold the land again. As this process continued, cohesive Amish communities or settlements began to appear, first in Pennsylvania and then in other states, specifically Ohio, Indiana, and Illinois.

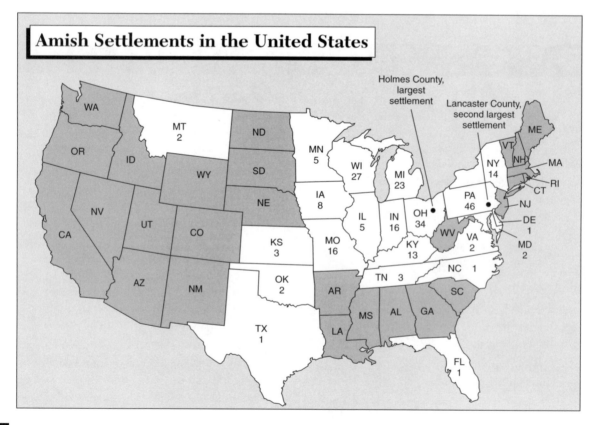

Amish Settlements in the United States

Holmes County, largest settlement

Lancaster County, second largest settlement

WA

MT 2

ND

OR

ID

WY

SD

MN 5

WI 27

MI 23

NY 14

ME

VT

NH

MA

RI

CT

NV

UT

CO

NE

IA 8

IL 5

IN 16

OH 34

PA 46

NJ

CA

KS 3

MO 16

KY 13

WV

VA 2

DE 1

MD 2

AZ

NM

OK 2

AR

TN 3

NC 1

SC

TX 1

LA

MS

AL

GA

FL 1

Today, there are more than 220 Amish settlements in 22 states, and one Canadian province. The size of these settlements varies from a couple of households to an area as large as several counties. The largest settlement in terms of population is Holmes County, Ohio, with thirty thousand Amish residents. Lancaster County, Pennsylvania, the most well-known settlement, has eighteen thousand Amish residents.

Reasons to Move

Although some settlements have existed for many years, a sizable majority—about two-thirds—are less than thirty years old. Amish families pack their belongings and move, sometimes across the country, to start or join a settlement for many reasons. One of the most common reasons is the need for cheaper farmland. The Amish population doubles in size approximately every twenty years and each succeeding generation needs to find land suitable to maintain an Amish lifestyle. In some older, established areas, such as Lancaster County, there is very little farmland available and the land that is available is beyond the price range of most young Amish. As a result, every year Amish families move to new territories where land is plentiful and affordable.

Other reasons for moving are cited in *The Amish in Their Own Words*, compiled by Brad Igou:

1. To establish a plainer church discipline.

2. To establish a more modern church discipline.

3. To escape church problems.

4. To improve youth problems.

Amish communities double in size every twenty years, increasing the necessity of more affordable farmland.

5. To avoid urban crowding and the regulations it imposes on rural people.

6. To better oneself financially.[25]

For all these reasons, Amish settlements come and go. Between 1974 and 1984, for example, fifteen settlements were started and disbanded. Although there have been attempts to establish settlements in such far-flung places as Belize and Paraguay, nearly all new settlements are founded in the United States. Families are important in Amish culture and even though young people move away to start new settlements, they generally try to stay as close as they can to their relatives. States with rising Amish populations include Wisconsin, New York, and Missouri. These areas have rolling land that is ideally suited to Amish horse farming. But southern states, such as Texas, Virginia, and North Carolina, have also seen the establishment of communities in the last few decades, in part because land there is relatively inexpensive.

"We Can Make a Good Life Here"

In the late 1990s, two Amish families started a settlement near the small town of Cisco, Texas. In all, nine members of the Petersheim family and five from the Johnathan family moved from Pennsylvania to rugged west Texas because of the availability of cheap land and an open, rural landscape. "We felt this was the kind of place where you could be one with nature," Ivan Petersheim told a Texas newspaper. "The land was nice, and we feel we can make a good life here. We welcome the challenge of living in nature."[26]

Living with nature for the Petersheims means a two-hour horse-and-buggy ride into town along a busy highway. Local residents, concerned for the safety of the Amish, installed yellow caution signs with an outline of a horse and buggy to warn motorists of the slow-moving vehicles. Townspeople also worry that the extreme heat of the region could cause trouble for the Petersheims, who do not have air conditioning. Helen Gaeta, a member of the chamber of commerce, who brings supplies and groceries to the Amish family, says, "They are wonderfully nice people, and we want to make sure they survive out there. We are constantly looking for ways to make things easier for them without trying to change their lifestyle."[27]

But the Petersheims do not think they will have a problem surviving in the area. They have a vegetable garden and a low cost of living. "We appreciate how friendly everyone is." Ivan Petersheim says. "But we expect to be pretty self-sufficient out here. Maybe we will remind people a little about Texas history, when people used to live off the land."[28]

"We Wouldn't Leave"

Although Amish residents of Burkes Garden, Virginia, didn't have to deal with a harsh climate like that of west Texas, they nevertheless faced an uphill battle establishing a permanent settlement. During the 1990s five Amish families called Burkes Garden home, but by April 1999 all the Amish had left the area. The families had relocated to settlements in Indiana, Wisconsin, and other parts of Virginia. The Amish farms had done well in Burkes Garden. The last Amish farmer to auction off his property acknowledged he had made a good living there. But making money was not the main concern of the Amish residents, who had hoped to build a community that would endure for generations.

Unfortunately they never realized that goal. Non-Amish residents grabbed up farmland whenever it became available, making it impossible for the Amish to expand. Without additional farmland, new Amish families couldn't move in. Without new families, there weren't enough members to create a self-sustaining community, so the Amish residents moved elsewhere, even though they had been financially successful in Burkes Garden. As one Amish farmer put it: "If we were looking only for farmland, we wouldn't leave."[29]

Twenty to Thirty Families

In the areas where Amish communities do succeed, the society is organized into three basic units: settlement; church district, or congregation; and affiliation. The settlement comprises the entire occupied geographic area; the church district is a subdivision small enough so that members can visit each other easily by horse and buggy. Church districts are also limited in size because worship services are held in members' homes instead of meetinghouses. On average, a church district includes about two hundred people. An Amish bishop, asked how many people belonged to his church, responded: "About

Because so many Amish people have the same first and last name, it is sometimes difficult to know exactly whom people are talking about. In all, there are only 126 family names used among the 150,000 Amish. The most common surname is Miller. Other typical Amish surnames include King, Yoder, Fisher, Troyer, and Bontrager.

The Amish also use relatively few first names. Five to 10 percent of all males are named John and 10 percent of all females are named Mary. Other popular male names include Eli, Amos, and Levi. Rebecca, Katie, Sarah, and Annie are favorite female names.

In the book *Sarah's Seasons*, writer Martha Moore Davis learns from Sarah Fisher, an Amish woman, several ways by which the Amish identify one another.

Families are referred to by the last name made plural—Fishers—or by the father's first name made plural; for example, "Elis came to visit" means that Eli's whole family visited. Sarah often refers to her own parents and siblings as "Dads" or "Pops." Sometimes she adds a middle initial following a first name to ensure accurate identification; for example, "Norman Ts" refers specifically to Norman T and his family, as distinguished from another Norman and his family.

As another way to clarify, a family or the member of that family is sometimes referred to with two names, the first the father's name and the second the mother's name. "Jonah Claras" refers to the family in which the father's name is Jonah and the mother's name is Clara. The singular form, "Jonah Clara," refers to the woman named Clara who is married to Jonah.

twenty to thirty families. That's about how many we can fit into one house, and it's still few enough for everyone to know each other's name. That's important to us."[30] Because everyone knows everyone else, there is no need for the Amish to keep membership lists or rolls.

Church districts are self-governing. The Amish don't have a central headquarters that sets standards and policies. Instead, each district determines its own set of rules for members to follow. As a result, church districts are not always in agreement about issues such as how strictly to enforce shunning or how much technology to use. Districts that share beliefs, however, form an affiliation and are considered to be in "fellowship" with each other. Young people may marry only someone from their own district or from a district that is in "fellowship."

Religious Splits

Before 1860 the Amish church was one group and there were no affiliations. But in 1862, the church split in two. The more conservative members formed the Old Order Amish, while liberal members called themselves Amish-Mennonite and eventually merged with the Mennonite Church. The Old Order Amish is the most common affiliation and accounts for roughly 75 percent of all Amish. In 1913, the Old Order Amish split, creating a new group called the Swartzentruber Amish. The Swartzentruber Amish steadfastly oppose the use of motorized farm technology, such as tractors. They also do not use modern conveniences, including indoor bathrooms and linoleum flooring.

More recently, the Amish church has split several times, each time yielding a new affiliation.

Although these affiliations still follow the basic tenets of the Amish faith, they do differ from the more traditional groups. For instance, the New Order Amish are more tolerant of modern technology and members can have linoleum floors and indoor plumbing and use tractors for hauling goods. The Beachy Amish, another affiliation, can own automobiles and conduct their worship services in English instead of German. Even though allowable technology and behavior is different for each of these affiliations, the members in each group are expected to adhere to their community's *Ordnung*.

Leadership Roles

Amish leadership is responsible for ensuring that members follow the rules and regulations. There are three levels of leadership in every Amish church district: a bishop, two ministers, and a deacon. Qualities considered important for church leadership include humility and good farm management.

The leaders have different responsibilities within the community. The bishop is the spiritual head of the congregation. In addition to preaching at the Sunday worship service, the

Different Amish leaders have different roles in the community. Here, a minister reads the prayer at a Pennsylvania church service.

bishop performs baptisms, communion, marriages, and funerals. The ministers take turns preaching at the worship service and help pass out wine and bread at the communion service. And the deacon oversees the funds that have been collected to help the poor. He also assists during the communion service.

Chosen by Chance

A church leadership role lasts a lifetime. Selecting a leader relies, in part, on chance, although the Amish believe God plays a role as well. When a bishop dies, his position will be filled by one of the ministers. When there is a vacancy for a minister or deacon, however, baptized members, both men and women, are asked to choose a candidate, although only married men can hold a church office. A man would never campaign or seek a leadership role, as that would show a lack of *Demut*, or humility. By the same token, a man would never announce he had a calling and attend a seminary. To receive religious training would be a sure sign of *Hochmut*, or pride.

During the selection process, each member whispers to the bishop the name of the man he wants to nominate. The bishop keeps a tally of names and if a man receives at least two nominations (three in some districts) his name is thrown into a lot. A candidate cannot take his name out of the lot for any reason, including illness or hardship, as this would be bad luck.

Once the list of names has been determined, the bishop takes a slip of paper and writes a Bible verse on it. He then places the slip of paper in a hymnal, which is put on a table with other hymnals. The candidates are brought into the room and each selects a hymnal from the table. One by one, they open their hymnals looking for the slip of paper. The man who opens the hymnal and finds the Bible verse will become the new church leader. The Amish be-

The Amish believe their religious and community leaders are chosen, in part, by God.

lieve that the man who selects the hymnal with the slip of paper is God's choice for the job.

When a new leader is chosen, the congregation responds not with rejoicing and celebration but with laments and weeping. Everyone feels sorry for that man because of the heavy burden the office places on him and his family. Church leaders receive no pay and must put in many long hours, in addition to their farm work, to take care of church business. In a letter to a new minister, an old minister explains some of the hardships that come with the job:

> You will never be the same again. . . . It will not seem fair that your neighbor can go ahead and get his chores done while you stand and explain some church decision to a

member who questions the decision. The same is true when your neighbor eats a good warm bowl of soup after a hard day of work while you skip supper because the deacon came to take you with him on the thankless task of visiting an erring member.[31]

Shunning

One of the most important responsibilities of church leaders is to ensure that members follow the church's rules and regulations. When a member does defy the *Ordnung*, however, the leaders and congregation work together to persuade him or her to stop the objectionable behavior. For minor offenses, such as attending a dance or wearing jewelry, church leaders may only ask the erring member to correct the behavior and make a public confession. But for serious offenses, including buying an automobile or getting a divorce, the punishment is more drastic. These types of violations require an automatic six-week ban against the offender. During this time, the banned member may attend church but must eat meals at a table separate from family and friends. If at the end of the six-week period, the offending member refuses to admit guilt in front of the congregation, he or she will be excommunicated, or thrown out of the church indefinitely. When this happens, the other church members will shun, or socially avoid, the wrongdoer, until that individual offers to make amends for his or her actions. The erring member is treated as an outcast and no longer part of the community.

In *Amish Society*, John Hostetler tells the story of a twenty-three-year-old Amish man who was excommunicated and shunned because he purchased an automobile. The punishment meant that he could not eat at the same table with his parents or take his sisters to church services, even if he took them in a horse and buggy. Eventually, his parents found his presence in the home intolerable and asked him to leave. Hostetler quotes the young man as saying: "I had to move away from home or my parents could not take communion. My parents were afraid that younger persons in the family would be led astray. They didn't exactly chase me off the place, but I was no longer welcome at home."[32]

Helping Each Other

Just as the Amish band together to uphold the *Ordnung*, they also support and help one another when a member is in need. The Amish do not purchase health, life, or property insurance, which they view as "worldly." They reject as security the financial compensation of an impersonal insurance policy; rather, the Amish put their faith in God and their community, and their own resources of time and money. When disaster or illness strikes, a far-reaching network of support takes over. If a farmer is sick, for example, his neighbors or relatives make sure his crops are harvested. If a barn burns, the entire community spends a day rebuilding it. If a child needs an expensive medical procedure, members from several Amish communities will pitch in to pay for it.

Times of trouble aren't the only occasions when the Amish support each other. Quiltings, weddings, and school fundraising events all require people to volunteer their time and talents. A writer who was reared Amish recalls how farmers helped each other during threshing season. (In the threshing process, the grains and seed of harvested crops are removed from the straw and shaft.) "Each summer, thrashing [threshing] was an anticipated community event. From six to ten farmers in a neighborhood formed what was called a thrashing ring. When a farmer's job was completed, the thrashing machine and crew moved on to the next farm."[33]

Threshing is hard work, but the Amish participate willingly. A participant recalls that on one particular day, the temperature was nearly ninety degrees. The members of the Amish threshing crew took to the fields

Barn raising is one of many community efforts in which the Amish happily offer each other support.

A Million Ants

In a 1992 *Life* magazine article entitled "Fire, Hope, and Charity . . ." writer Jeanne Marie Laskas reported the story of six Amish barns that had been torched in secluded Kishacoquillas Valley, Pennsylvania. The fires, set by unknown arsonists, killed 139 cows and 38 horses. Sam Z. Yoder's ninety-year-old barn was one of those destroyed. Almost immediately after the incident, the Amish community began to rebuild Yoder's barn.

People from the outside world wonder how the Amish can live such secluded rule-bound lives. But such doubters have never seen an Amish barn-raising. You watch all those men dressed alike in their dark clothes and straw hats, all crawling so nimbly over the fresh wood standing against the sky, and you can't help but notice what they look like.

They look like ants.

It isn't such a bad image. One ant can't do much but a million ants working together can perform miracles. An Amish barn-raising is a belief system in action: Sacrifice individuality—forget about your self, your clothes, your hair, your creative longings—in favor of the common good.

A visitor from New York City walks up to Sam Z. She has been shaking her head all day in disbelief, watching this barn emerge. "If my house in Brooklyn burned down," she says, "I don't think my neighbors would come around to rebuild it."

Sam Z. ponders that piece of information, then says, "We would."

Amish men collectively erect a barn.

and did not relent until the job was completed. He says:

> The wagon stopped. . . . Somberly and silently, the men spilled to the ground and began thrusting their forks and ripping [the shocks of grain] apart. The shocks dissociated into sheaves, bundles of wheat stalks each tied, like a large broom head, with a piece of twine around the center. . . . With a deft flick, the men would catch two or three sheaves on the tines of the pitchfork and scoop them up and over the side of the wagon.[34]

But the Amish do more than volunteer their labor to help others. Twice a year, members donate money to the district's "poor fund," a collection used to help members who cannot meet their expenses. "The deacon holds a black bag open at the door as we go out after the [communion] service," an Amish woman explains. "No one knows how much anyone puts in. That's the money we use to help any member who is old or sick and maybe doesn't have enough to live on."[35]

Such actions prove that the Amish are a community, rather than a collection of individuals. They value this ideal and do everything they can—whether as leaders or community members—to maintain that interconnected way of life.

CHAPTER 3

Patterns of Worship

Religious ceremonies are solemn occasions in Amish society. Ritual events such as baptisms and weddings mark the stages of an individual's life. Like much of Amish life, ceremonies and rituals follow weekly and seasonal patterns. Worship services and visiting takes place on Sunday. Communion and council meetings are held in the spring and fall. Baptism occurs in early fall, while November and December are wedding months.

The Preaching Service

Sunday is a day of worship, rest, and visiting. The day's activities begin early, around five o'clock in the morning. Although the Amish do no unsanctioned work on Sunday, they must take care of their farm animals, so the day of rest includes morning and evening chores. As one writer notes: "Sunday is a day of anticipation in Amish society. It makes no difference whether it is a warm, sunny morning or a blustery, winter day, the Amish father, mother, and all the children in the family hustle around, get the cows milked, and by eight o'clock are on their way to the preaching service."[36]

Actually, worship services take place every other Sunday. The origin of this schedule is unknown; most Amish simply accept it as the way things have always been done. Church attendance is not optional; all members are expected to participate.

Depending on how far they live from the place of worship, families either walk or drive a buggy. The Sunday service is important to the Amish because it brings everyone together. Sociologist John Hostetler, who grew up Amish, describes how members feel as they see their neighbors approaching: "The sight of a dozen carriages turning single-file into the long farm lane, and the sound of still other horses trotting on the hard surface over the hill, evokes deep sentiments among the gathering community."[37]

The Amish do not build dedicated church buildings; instead, they hold worship services in members' homes on a rotating basis. Generally, a family will host one or two Sunday services a year. Amish homes are specially constructed to accommodate the congregation. Their houses include wide doors or movable partitions that allow members to view the preacher regardless of where they are sitting. Special wagons carry folding benches and hymnals to the home of the host family. Furniture inside the home is moved or temporarily stored to make room for the long benches. In summer months, services are sometimes held in barns that are large enough to contain the congregation.

Getting Ready

There is a great deal of work to be done when it is a family's turn to host the service. Hostetler describes the preparation during the week before the service: "The mundane work takes on ritual significance as stables are emptied of manure and carpets are removed from the house. The burden of the work falls on the woman, since the house must be cleaned, the furniture rearranged, the stove blackened, and the ornamental china washed."[38] On the day of the service, sons of the host family help visitors unhitch their horses and put them into the barn, where there is plenty of hay on hand.

On Saturday, the day before the service, neighboring women drop by to help prepare food that will be served for Sunday lunch. The menu is always the same and includes food that can be easily made in advance. A typical Sunday lunch menu would include homemade

The Amish hold Sunday services in community members' homes. Here, carriages are parked near an Amish church meeting.

bread with spreads such as jelly, apple butter, and molasses; cheese cubes; pickles and pickled beets; Schnitz pie made with dried apple slices; coffee and tea.

"Children Are *Welcome*"

The Sunday service can last from three to four hours, and there is no break. During this time, the congregation sits on hard, backless benches, except for elderly members who are given chairs. Men and women sit in separate sections which offer equal views of the preaching area. There are no Sunday school classes so children attend the service with their parents. Boys sit with their fathers and girls with their mothers.

The Amish believe that "church ought to be one place where children are *welcome*,"[39] so communities encourage youngsters, even tiny

Women take a break from preparing the food they will serve after the Sunday worship service.

The Amish separate women and men during church services.

babies, to attend. Parents give their children small, quiet toys, such as a string with beads or buttons on it, and during the service, snacks, such as crackers, are passed around to youngsters. Mothers with infants sit in the kitchen so they can nurse and tend to their babies.

The *Ausbund*

Singing is an integral part of the service. The Amish hymnal, the *Ausbund*, is the oldest hymnal still in use. When it was first printed in 1564 it contained 53 hymns. Today the *Ausbund* includes 140 hymns. Most of the original hymns were written in 1535 by a group of Anabaptists who were imprisoned in Bavaria for their religious beliefs. As a result, the hymns describe suffering and loneliness. Yet since the people writing the songs were a pious group, the hymns also reflect the joy of salvation and eternal life.

An unusual feature of the *Ausbund* is that only the lyrics are printed. There is no musical notation in the book. This means the melodies must be learned by ear and memorized. Amish hymns are sung slowly and in unison. During the service, a song leader picks the pitch and sings the first line before the rest of the congregation joins in. The amount of time

In his autobiography, *Dust Between My Toes*, physician Wayne Weaver describes his earliest memory of attending an Old Order Amish church service when he was about three years old.

On this Sunday, I was sitting on Father's lap and fell asleep. Later I awoke, lying on the bench, with my head in his lap. The sermon was going on in German. The preacher's voice was coming from the direction of the granary. When I couldn't identify its source, my young mind concluded it was *da Gute Mon* talking from the granary. Amish children call God *"da Gute Mon."* This can best be translated as *benevolent creator* and *Lord*. I don't recall being greatly puzzled. It seems I was more bewildered later when I learned the voice wasn't God's.

it takes to sing a song varies from one area to another. The hymn "Loblied," for example, is the second hymn sung in every church district. How long it takes to sing the hymn, however, depends on how conservative the church district is. The more conservative, the longer it takes. A conservative congregation can take nearly thirty minutes to sing the hymn, while a more liberal congregation will sing it in eleven minutes.

Plain Service

Amish religious services, as is everyday life, are simple and plain, a fact that reflects basic Amish values. There are no ushers, flowers, or altars at the Sunday service. There are also no pianos or organs to accompany the singing; the Amish believe that the voice is a gift from God but that musical instruments are not. Additionally, the Amish contend that musical accompaniment draws attention away from the words themselves. According to one community member, "Instrumental music tends to draw attention to itself through its natural beauty, distracts our thoughts from the meaning of the words we sing, and entertains us rather than glorifying God."[40]

Order of the Sunday Worship Service

The order of the Sunday service has changed little over time and varies only slightly from one church district to another. As the worshipers arrive at the host family's home, the men and women gather in groups outside. When it's time to begin, the men and women enter the house through different doors. First to enter are the ordained and married men, followed by the women and girls. The last to come in are the unmarried men and boys, who often wait until the final minute to make their appearance.

The service begins with hymn singing. While the congregation sings, the ministers gather in another room of the house to decide on the order of their sermons. A typical service begins with an opening, or introductory sermon, followed by a Bible reading; then a main sermon, which lasts more than an hour, and concludes with another Bible reading. After the preachers have finished, visiting ministers or members of the congregation give testimonies that support the ideas expressed in the main sermon. Their discussion is followed by a kneeling prayer, a blessing, and a closing hymn. At the conclusion of the service, the congregation disbands, starting with the youngest first and continuing upward in age, with the eldest leaving last.

Lunch follows the service but is usually served in three or four shifts to accommodate the large number of people. Ordained men, married men, and visitors always eat in the first shift, and young children always eat last. Women and girls set the tables and clean up after the meal. After the meal, members spend time visiting with families before leaving for home around two or three o'clock.

Amish worship services are structured formally and include hymn singing, prayer, and bible readings.

Buggies line the street after an Amish church service.

Baptism

Once a year in the fall, the church service takes on a special significance when it includes a baptismal rite. The Amish do not believe in infant baptism because they think that joining the church should be a voluntary decision. For this reason, members are baptized when they are in their late teens or early twenties. An Amish minister explains, "That way you have time to think about such an important decision, one that will affect the rest of your life."[41]

For the Amish, baptism is a turning point. After individuals are baptized, they are considered adult members of the community. And being an adult member means that a person must act responsibly and follow the rules and regulations of the church district. An observer who lived with the Amish for a time notes that baptism "was a coming of age ritual, a rite of passage. Once a young person chose to be baptized, everything changed." [42]

"Running Around" Time

Baptism ends a period known as *rumschpringes*, or "running around" time. From the age of sixteen to about twenty-four, Amish youth are allowed to "run around," meaning they are permitted to experiment with "worldly" practices, such as smoking, drinking alcohol, and owning a car. Amish parents hope that during this time, their children will learn to appreciate the culture in which they have grown up and choose to remain in it for the rest of their lives.

Young people who decide not to be baptized must leave the community. However, they do not have to sever all ties with family and friends, for they have not broken any vows; the church cannot excommunicate or shun anyone who has not been baptized. Hostetler describes his own decision not to be baptized in his family's church: "I did not want to take a vow I could not keep, nor take a vow that implied social avoidance in case I could not live by Amish standards. Consequently, on the day my chums began their instruction for baptism, I drove my horse and buggy to the nearby Mennonite church."[43] Despite the strict rules, the vast majority of young people choose to be baptized and join the church. Only about 15 to 20 percent of Amish youth leave.

The young people who decide to stay in the Amish community must attend a series of instruction classes that last from May to August. The purpose of the classes is to prepare the baptismal candidates for church membership. In September, when the baptismal

Amish youth, like this girl are expected to make their own decisions regarding baptism. Those who choose not to be baptized, though, must leave the community.

rite is held, the candidates pledge their willingness to follow their church district's *Ordnung*. At the end of the baptismal rite, the bishop takes the hand of each candidate and offers a greeting of welcome into the church. Being a full member of the church means the person can participate in the communion service and vote on church matters. It also means the person can get married, for only baptized individuals can be married in the church.

Sometimes though, church members question the young people's motives for deciding to be baptized since certain privileges are reserved for those members who participate in the ceremony. According to one Amish writer: "When I was taking instruction for baptism, there were several in my group who were not permitted to date until they were baptized. On the evening of the day of their baptism, all of them dated. How sad that they should cast a shadow of suspicion upon their motives for being baptized."[44]

Council Meetings and Communion

In addition to baptismal rites, the Amish participate in other ceremonies to help promote harmony in the community. Communion, for example, is held twice a year, in the spring and the fall. Two weeks before the communion service, all baptized church members gather for a council meeting or "preparatory service." During the council meeting, members must reaffirm their agreement to abide by the *Ordnung*. In the book *The Riddle of Amish Culture*, a member explains the process: "Two of the ministers go around, one with the men and one with the women, and they go around and ask each one, 'Are you agreed?' and everybody says, 'I'm agreed,' and you better be, too!"[45] The council meeting

is also the time when members resolve any disagreements they have with each other. The congregation cannot have the communion service until all disputes among themselves are settled.

About a week before the communion service, one day is set aside for fasting. This ritual is mostly symbolic, as the fasting does not last for the entire day. Instead, baptized members do not eat breakfast and spend the morning in quiet reflection.

Foot Washing and a Holy Kiss

Once the congregation is "at peace" with the *Ordnung* and each other, the communion ceremony can take place. Communion includes a lengthy sermon and a foot-washing rite. The foot-washing practice follows the command in the Bible that says, "Ye also ought to wash each other's feet." As part of the ritual, the deacon brings in buckets of warm water and towels. Men are in one room and women in another. Members sing as they take off their shoes and socks. They then go in pairs up to the buckets of water, where they wash and dry each other's feet. This ritual is meant to show humility, for as one member writes, "Our attitude toward our brother [or sister] must be that of a servant, feeling ourselves of less importance than the one whose feet we wash."[46] After the ritual, the foot-washing partners give each other a "holy kiss," which is a quick kiss on the cheek considered a symbol of Christian love and goodwill.

For Adults Only

Although children attend the Sunday worship service, they do not go to the council meeting

Amish teenagers go on a chaperoned date, in the young man's bachelor buggy.

or the communion service. Both of these ceremonies are intended for baptized adult members only. Since the communion service lasts for eight hours and the council meeting goes on until mid-afternoon, and the Amish believe it is unreasonable to expect a child to sit still for such a long time.

Consequently, these special days mean that parents and children have a rare break from each other. As sociologist John Hostetler explains:

> Amish children look forward to these occasions because they may spend the whole day with children of the neighborhood and be free from adult supervision. . . . Parents also look forward to these occasions, because they are a change from the usual routine. Parents enjoy the liberty of attending services without squirming youngsters by their side."[47]

Singings

Despite these rare and welcomed breaks, the family is the heart of Amish society. Thus, choosing a marriage partner is an important decision. Young people must find a suitable mate within their district or a district that is in "fellowship" with theirs. The typical age for both men and women to marry is between twenty and twenty-five. A few years before, teenagers start looking for potential partners at Sunday night singings, which take place in the home of the family that hosted the worship service that week. Singings bring together young people of dating age from districts that are in fellowship with one another. At the event, the young men sit on one side of a table and the young women on the other, and they take turns leading hymn singing. The hymn singing stops around ten o'clock but the young people stay for another hour or so talking and

Although courtship rituals are changing and becoming more modern, some Amish communities still observe traditional practices. In *Amish Society*, author John Hostetler describes how young couples keep their relationships secret from family and friends. In this passage Hostetler begins by telling how a young man prepares for a date.

When Saturday evening comes, he dresses in his best; he makes little ado about his departure and attempts to give the impression to his younger brothers and sisters that he is going to town on business.

Before entering the home of his girl, he makes sure that the "old folks" [the girl's parents] have retired. Standard equipment for every young Amishman of courting age is a good flashlight. When the girl sees the light focused on her window, she knows that her boy friend has arrived, and she quietly goes downstairs to let him in. The couple may be together in the home until the early morning hours on such occasions. They often play games and enjoy the company of another couple. The clatter of horses' hoofs on hard-surface roads in the early hours of the morning is evidence of young suitors coming home.

socializing. At the end of the evening, if a boy is interested in a girl, he will offer to take her home in his "bachelor" buggy.

It's a Secret

After a couple starts dating, the pair usually sees each other on the Saturday night when there is no church service for the girl the following morning. Dating couples don't go to the movies or out to eat at a restaurant; instead, they visit relatives or get together with friends. Dating has traditionally been secretive in Amish society but that has been changing in recent years. Even so, young men and women are reluctant to talk about the person they are dating for fear of being teased by family and friends. As a sociologist notes, "Among themselves, young people seldom refer to their boy or girl friends by name. The pronoun 'he' or 'she' is used instead."[48]

Dating might be more open these days but engagements are still private matters. An Amish couple doesn't throw an engagement party and a man doesn't give a woman a ring. In fact, community members will learn that a couple is planning to get married only when the news is "published," or announced, in church about a month before the event. Until then, people can only guess that there might be impending nuptials. Neighbors, for example, will take note if a family plants lots of celery in the spring, as extra celery might mean that a daughter plans to marry. The bride's parents are responsible for the wedding dinner and an Amish wedding menu includes a lot of celery.

Go-Between

After a couple has decided they want to marry, the young man and woman tell their parents, but there is no official mention in the community of their plans until the end of the harvest season in the fall. At that time, the prospective groom visits a deacon of his own choosing. He brings with him a letter witnessed by the church leaders that says he is a member in good standing with the church. The young man will then ask the deacon to act as a *Schteckliman*, or go-between, with his girlfriend's family. The *Schteckliman* then goes to the home of the bridegroom's fiancée and verifies her wishes for marriage. In addition, he obtains the consent of her parents.

When this task is accomplished, the marriage will be "published" at the Sunday service. However, on this day, the prospective bride and groom do not attend the service. Instead, the young couple has dinner together while their families are at church. In the coming weeks, the groom often stays at his fiancée's home to help her family with wedding preparations.

Once the engagement is official, a wedding day must be selected. Most weddings take place in November or December, and Tuesday and Thursday are popular wedding days as this ensures that no preparation or cleanup work will be done on Sunday. When the date has been chosen, nearby guests will receive a personal invitation or a handwritten note while a postcard or letter notifies out-of-town relatives.

Wedding Clothes

The Amish bridal party's wardrobe and accessories are plain and simple. There are no wedding rings, flowers, or veils. An Amish bride sews her own dress, which traditionally is dark blue. Under the dress, she wears a special wedding stocking that has a decorative border along the top edge of the band. She also wears a white cape and apron, which she will pack away after the wedding. These will not be worn again during her lifetime. By custom, Amish women are buried wearing their wedding cape and apron. The bride's two female attendants sew their dresses out of the same material as the bride's dress and all three wear prayer caps. The groom and his attendants sport black suits with white shirts and black bow ties.

The Day Before

The day before the wedding, married couples acting as helpers arrive at the bride's house early in the morning. They will help prepare food for as many as two hundred guests and get the house ready. Some couples, called roast cooks, are in charge of roasting the chickens.

A couple takes a buggy ride after their marriage ceremony.

Others are potato cooks, responsible for making the mashed potatoes and gravy. Generally, women bake doughnuts and pies, peel potatoes, and wash the dishes. In addition, the men clean celery and make sure there is enough hot water available. A wedding is one of the few occasions when an Amish man helps in the kitchen.

Exchanging Vows

An Amish wedding is an elaborate all-day affair. In a morning church service, the couple exchanges vows. These wedding vows are taken seriously. For the Amish, marriage is a lifetime commitment, and divorce, which goes against the *Ordnung*, is not allowed. During the wedding service, the bishop stresses that marriage is permanent and asks the young couple if they are ready to become lifelong partners.

Following the service, there is a noontime dinner. In *Driving the Amish*, Jim Butterfield notes that the food served at a wedding includes "pan-baked chicken, heaps of mashed potatoes, dressing and gravy, lettuce salad, platters of cheese and bologna, loaves of bread and spreads (peanut butter and honey, apple butter, jelly), bowls of fruit, date pudding, frosted cake, two kinds of pie, and ice cream!"[49] When the meal is over, guests sing and play games, such as darts. Later in the evening, another meal will be served before guests start to head home around ten o'clock.

Usually the church service and the reception that follows are held in the bride's home. Throughout the wedding, the bridal party sits at the *Eck*, or "corner table," in the most visible corner of the living room. The *Eck* also holds the fancy dishes and wedding cakes, which can be homemade or store bought.

Although the food is plentiful, very few gifts are brought to an Amish wedding. The gifts a bride does receive are practical and include items such as canned foods, tablecloths, clocks, and farm tools.

A Wedding in the House

Grace H. Kaiser practiced medicine in eastern Pennsylvania for twenty-eight years. In her book *Detour*, she describes her experiences as a woman doctor among the Amish. In this excerpt from the book, Kaiser recalls her reaction as she reached the home where an Amish wedding was taking place.

A wall of hot air bearing odors of cooked onions and celery, roast chicken and the stuffiness of a crowd met us at the open door. The Fisher house had changed. The stone farmhouse had always seemed large, but on this wedding day it rivaled the barn floor. The varnished wooden partitions between [the] bedroom, the parlor, the large kitchen, even into [the] frame end of the house, had been removed to make one large room. Beds had been taken down, bureaus and cupboards taken out or pushed against the wall. Parlor rugs were gone exposing wide pine boards. Only the usual three space heaters remained. I wondered if they were needed or if the knurls of black-garbed women sitting about chatting in Pennsylvania Dutch would have warmed the room.

When an Amish person dies, community members take over the chores of the bereaved family.

Newlyweds

The bride and groom spend their first night together at her family's house so that they can get up early the next morning and help clean and wash laundry. Instead of going on a honeymoon, the couple visits relatives for the first weeks of their marriage. These visits, which can last for a day or overnight, give the newlyweds an opportunity to talk, play games, and do needlework with their relatives. The hosts give the couple a wedding gift during the visit.

Not until the following spring will the bridal couple settle into a home of their own. This allows the couple to go visiting and acquire the items they will need to furnish a house, although the bride's parents provide the major pieces of furniture, such as a refrigerator and stove, bed-room suite, kitchen table, hutch, and cupboard, as a part of their daughter's dowry. The couple will keep these items all their lives and when they die, the pieces will be sold at auction rather than divided up in a will so that all their children can have an equal chance at acquiring them.

Funerals

If a wedding is the ceremony that brings the Amish together in joy, funerals bring them together in mourning. Even so, the Amish view illness, old age, and death as natural parts of life, and families accept the death of a loved one because they believe it is God's will. For example, an Amish mother, whose baby died shortly after being born, wrote: "Of course, all the time the question 'Why?' comes to our minds. But we should not expect to be able to understand everything in this life, and should never put a question mark where God has put a period."[50]

Although the *Ordnung* does not prohibit the Amish from going to hospitals, family members usually take care of the elderly and sick at home. When someone becomes seriously ill, family and friends keep a vigil. And when someone dies, the news spreads quickly throughout the community and neighbors step in and take over farm and household chores for the bereaved family.

In most cases, a funeral is held three days after a death and takes place in the home of the family of the deceased. The deceased is dressed all in white and laid out in a plain, wooden coffin. At the funeral service, the minister speaks about the person who has died and reads from the Bible.

After the sermon concludes, the coffin is taken by wagon to the burial site. Family and friends form a procession to the graveyard. Most established Amish communities have their own cemeteries, where small, plain markers serve as tombstones. At the gravesite, the mourners sing a scriptural verse, such as:

> Good night, you who are grieving,
> And out of love for me now weep![51]

While the group is singing, the pallbearers throw shovels of dirt into the open grave until it begins to fill. Following the burial, the mourners gather for a meal.

Amish ceremonies and ritual—funerals, weddings, rites of passage—allow members to reaffirm their shared beliefs. These events bring order and continuity to a community that respects tradition. These events also serve as meeting places for families and friends, who cherish the time they spend with each other.

A Time for Everything

In Amish society, there is a time and a place for everything. Every morning the farm animals are fed. Every Monday the laundry is washed and hung to dry. Every spring the fields are planted. Life has a slow, predictable rhythm, and there is no reason to hurry to get a job done. Instead, it's more important to do a job well. The Amish do their work the old-fashioned way without the help of cars or electricity because they believe modern technology would speed up their lives too much and leave them with little time to spend with their families.

The Family

The family is the heart of Amish society, reflecting the belief that parents are responsible for training children to live the Amish way. In an excerpt from *Family Life* magazine, a writer explains how working together helps

Amish children spend a great deal of time with their parents, from whom they learn the necessary skills for running a farm or household.

strengthen the family: "Our very lives center around our families and our children. . . . In our way of life, children are useful, needed, and wanted."[52]

Compared with non-Amish families, the typical Amish family spends a great deal of time together. Most of that time is spent in work-related activities, such as preserving food or plowing a field. In this way, Amish parents teach their children the skills needed to manage a household or run a farm.

Birth

As a result, the Amish view children as a blessing. A child is a welcome addition to the family and community. Children are an extra pair of hands to help around the farm and home, and every child is a potential future member of the church. For this reason, the birth of a baby is a joyous event. Although Amish women may choose to give birth in a hospital, most women have babies at home with the assistance of a midwife.

There are no special ceremonies to mark the birth. Because the Amish don't believe in infant baptism, there are no godparents. There also are no baby showers. Parents think that expensive or fanciful gifts, such as fancy clothes, given at a shower are unnecessary. Young children are dressed in practical clothes similar to the styles worn by adults.

For the first few years of life, an Amish child is rarely left alone. Parents, older siblings, and relatives take turns comforting and holding babies. But at around two years old, children must start to learn responsibility. Parents assign preschool boys and girls simple tasks around the home or farm, such as gathering eggs. Thus, from a young age, children learn the value of work, a value the Amish believe in strongly. As an Amish writer explains, "Any child who doesn't grow up helping with dishes, or doing chores, or running errands—has been cheated out of a good start in life."[53]

Doctoring the Amish

The Amish have no restrictions on medical care and do use the services of hospitals and clinics. In rural Ohio, Dr. Elton Lehman has been servicing the Amish community for thirty-five years. Lehman, who was named Country Doctor of the Year in 1998, still makes house calls. Since most Amish don't have health insurance, Lehman offers discounts for patients who pay in cash. According to Katy Kelly's *USA Today* article entitled "'Doc Lehman' is a Bridge to Divergent Worlds," when families don't have enough money, Lehman accepts what they can give. "We have a quilt I got for taking care of a fractured leg and a rocking chair that was partial payment for delivery of a baby," Lehman says.

Although the Amish will go to doctors, they prefer to use traditional folk medicines, which have been handed down over the years and passed from family to family. The Amish have home remedies to cure everything from colds to hives to athlete's foot. The book *Amish Folk Medicine* by Patrick Quillin includes remedies to cure acne, cold sores, coughs, and a list of other ailments. Some of the remedies use common household ingredients such as vinegar but others, like the one for earache, call for items that are difficult to find like fresh sheep's wool with the lanolin still intact.

Even young children are expected to help their families. This boy diligently picks strawberries from a patch.

"A Celebration of Togetherness"

The Amish work long and hard taking care of their homes, farms, and businesses, but they don't mind because they find meaning in their work. Families work together, helping each other accomplish tasks such as cleaning the house or plowing the field. In this way, a sociologist writes, work "becomes a celebration of togetherness."[54]

Wayne Weaver, a physician, was reared in the Old Order Amish faith. Although he eventually left the sect, Weaver recalls his childhood in rural Ohio as a pleasant one. For Weaver, work was a natural part of his life and even part of his play:

Following Father from the feed mill to the chicken house, then to the barn, was part of a preschool day, unless there was bad weather. Watering and feeding the livestock and chickens didn't seem monotonous to me. I remember playing around Father's desk when he did bookkeeping work. In the early years, a day included make-believe work, play, and imposed naps. In the house, besides play, watching sewing, baking, washing and ironing, and other household tasks was the main pastime.[55]

A married couple prepares meat for canning. Both partners have clear roles but neither is considered more important than the other.

Marriage Roles

In an Amish family, husband and wife have very clear roles. The husband is considered the head of the family but the wife has a strong voice in family decisions, such as where they will live. The wife may also help with record-keeping for the farm operations.

The mother takes care of the children's daily needs, cleans house, prepares food, and tends the yard and garden. Women also help in the fields during harvesting season and, when needed, paint a fence or milk a cow.

The father runs the farm or business and oversees the religious upbringing of the children. Although men rarely do household work, the Amish do not view women's work as sec-

ondary to men's, for to survive on a small farm the skills and input of both men and women are needed and valued. A writer in *Family Life*, an Amish magazine, notes, "The Bible teaches us clearly that men and women are equal. . . . Each has been assigned separate and distinct roles."[56] The man works to earn money while the woman uses her skills to live frugally and save money.

An Amish Homestead

Amish homes tend to be bigger than non-Amish homes partly because Amish families are typically large. The average family includes seven or eight children, and about 20 percent of Amish couples have ten or more children. Also, because the Amish hold their worship services in members' homes, a house must be large enough to contain the entire congregation, which can be as many as two hundred people. If an Amish family buys a home from an *Englisher*, they will tear out walls on the first floor to accommodate a large number of people.

Amish homes also need lots of land. Even nonfarming families still need room for a stable to keep their horses. This is how a visitor describes the setting of an Amish farm: "One long shed housed a buggy, a road car, a pony cart, a spring wagon, and a two-seated surrey with brakes operated by a foot pedal. A banty rooster and two little hens scratched around the barnyard. A black collie barked, and a gasoline motor pumped water because no breeze was spinning the windmill."[57]

In some cases, three generations live on one homestead, with the parents and children living in the main house and the grandparents residing in the "grandfather house," or *Gross-daddi Haus*. When the grandparents are ready to retire from farming, the youngest son and his wife move into their home and construct a smaller "grandfather house" alongside the main one. The grandparents will live there for the rest of their lives. They furnish the home with their own furniture and also keep a horse and buggy of their own so that they can have the freedom to come and go as they like. Amish grandparents can work as much or as little as they want, but generally, they help with the farm chores and look after small grandchildren.

Lighting the Darkness

The Amish have no electricity in their homes. It isn't that they believe electricity itself is a sin.

Rather, they worry that using electricity would connect them to the outside world. Since one of the major tenets of the faith is to live separate from others, the Amish prefer to use alternative systems to light their homes, including kerosene lamps, pressure lamps, gasoline lamps, and long-stemmed floor lamps with individual propane tanks. Regardless of the method, the Amish can't turn on lights with a flick of the switch. Instead, individuals must use considerable care to operate these lamps properly. In *Living Without Electricity*, authors Stephen Scott and Kenneth Pellman describe what happens in a typical Amish home that doesn't have electric lights when it's time for the children to go to bed:

Most Amish people do not use electrical appliances and, instead, rely on old-fashioned methods of cooking and baking.

After the evening prayer the two oldest children, Joe and Rachel, took flashlights and led their brothers and sisters upstairs to the bedrooms.

Rachel entered the girls' room and directed the beam of the flashlight to a lamp on a table beside the bed. She took the glass chimney from the lamp and got a wooden match from a small container. After striking the match she held the flame to the bit of kerosene-soaked wick protruding above the brass fixture. . . .

Rachel put the chimney back on the lamp and adjusted the wick with a small knob so that the flame was neither too low nor too high. If the flame were too high, it would smoke.

The younger girls snuggled into bed in the unheated room, but Rachel spent a few minutes reading and writing before blowing out the light.[58]

The Kitchen

Just as the Amish have found nonelectrical systems to light their homes, they also have found ways to cook without electricity. Kitchen appliances such as stoves, refrigerators, and water heaters, which normally are powered by electricity, are modified to operate using natural gas or kerosene. Gasoline- and diesel-powered motors are also used to power appliances. And instead of refrigerators, many Amish homes have old-fashioned iceboxes, which require chunks of ice to keep contents cold.

The Amish have also come up with innovative ways to heat and cook their food. Instead of electric ovens, they use kerosene-burning stoves or gas ranges using bottled gas. Some Amish

groups use wood-burning cooking stoves, which also help to warm the house. Scott and Pellman describe the steps an Amish mother takes to ensure the wood stove is ready for cooking:

> [Katie, the mother] pulled out the air intake level on its side. After pausing a moment to avoid getting a cloud of smoke in her face, she grasped the detachable handle protruding from the stove top and lifted the circular lid over the fire box. She was delighted to see an abundance of glowing embers. . . .

> Katie stirred the coals with an iron poker, then laid several sticks of wood on top of them. She replaced the lid of the stove and adjusted the damper controls on the side so that more air would pass over the fire.[59]

The Wash Cycle

In addition to her time-consuming kitchen duties, an Amish woman spends a great deal of time washing and drying clothes for her family. Although some Amish groups use only hand-operated washing machines, most use gasoline-powered wringer washers. The women then hang the wet clothes outdoors on a clothesline to dry.

For the most part, the Amish use of synthetic materials has eliminated the need for ironing. When clothes do require pressing, however, an Amish woman uses a metal iron that has been heated on the stove or a special iron that operates on pressurized gas.

Water

Both cooking and washing require water, and the Amish use several methods to get water

Even though Amish women still spend many hours washing clothes for their families, the use of synthetic material has eliminated the need for much ironing.

into their homes, including old-fashioned hand pumps. About half of all Amish homes use windmills, which pump water into large storage tanks. From there, the water flows by gravity down to the residence or barn. Homes that use windmills or pressurized water systems have indoor plumbing that is nearly identical to that of non-Amish homes.

Furnishings

The interior of an Amish home, like the people themselves, is plain and functional. Pegs on the wall hold coats and hats. Simple white tieback curtains hang in windows. Braided rugs cover wooden floors. Magazine and newspaper racks hold reading material. Amish homes are sparsely furnished. Most of the furniture is unpainted or painted wood made by Amish craftsman. Typical furniture includes rockers, chairs, china cabinets, beds, kitchen tables, secretaries, and chests of drawers. Amish homes have few decorations and those that they do display must also be practical. Wall calendars, quilts, and china are all useful items that bring flashes of color to the otherwise austere Amish home.

Garden Plots

The garden provides a splash of color outside the home. An Amish garden is big and includes many varieties of flowers, vegetables, and fruits. Although they grow an abundance of flowers throughout the spring and summer, the Amish do not bring cut flowers into the home. Instead, they leave the flowers outdoors where they can be viewed and enjoyed by everyone.

The typical Amish garden also has lots of cucumbers and red beets, which are served at the Sunday worship service. In addition, edibles such as strawberries, apples, potatoes, green beans, sweet potatoes, and broccoli are also grown. Some of the food is eaten fresh but much of it is preserved so it can be eaten throughout the year. An Amish woman may preserve as much as eight hundred quarts of fruits and vegetables a year.

Creative Expression

For Amish women, gardening offers a mix of work and pleasure. It is a way for them to express themselves, as is quilting. Because Amish homes have no central heating system, quilts provide much-needed warmth on cold winter nights. When a young woman gets married, she will begin her married life with anywhere from two to thirteen quilts. Some of these are ones she has made herself and kept in a hope chest, and others are a gift from her mother.

Amish quilts are known for their dark, simple designs. Women use old clothing scraps to make the quilts, which require many hours of stitching. Quilting can be tedious work but it's

Gardening yields abundant vegetables and fruits for canning and is a source of pleasure for most Amish women.

Quilting provides both an income for the community and a creative outlet for women.

one of the few ways an Amish woman can show her creativity. And in the normally reserved world of the Amish, quilt making also allows a woman to show her feelings for her family, since quilts are most often given to family members. As one observer noted of an Amish woman: "The extra hours she spent quilting tiny stitches expressed her love for the person who would receive the quilt."[60]

Quilting Bees

In late fall through early spring, during downtime on the farm, Amish women gather at each other's homes for quilting bees. A quilting bee brings friends and families together to spend a day gossiping and creating a quilted work of art.

Quilting Party

Author Louise Stoltzfus grew up in a Pennsylvanian Old Order Amish family. In her book *Amish Women*, Stoltzfus writes how, on her fortieth birthday, her mother suggested having a quilting party to complete a quilt that had been started by Stoltzfus's late grandmother, Mary, more than thirty years earlier.

I eagerly agreed, and we set out to bring a piece of Grandmother Mary's work to life. We invited all of the aunts to a two-day quilting, asking them to invite their own daughters and granddaughters.

Many arrived early with their quilting needles, thimbles, scissors, and covered dishes of food. Expert fingers guided threaded needles across the quilt as conversation flowed above it. Occasional jokes about people who quilt too slowly or too quickly prompted easy laughter. Stories of husbands and brothers and sons were interspersed with peals of mirth over someone's forgetfulness; "We're all getting older, you know."

. . . Questions about family problems sometimes halted the quilting as everyone stopped to look up and hear the story from an aunt or cousin or granddaughter. The easy camaraderie sometimes veiled the pain, but it also opened doors for healing. Talking seemed to help make the problems less imposing, less frightful.

When the two days were finished and the last stitches came together at the quilt's center, I took home a work of art, completed with four generations of needlework and love.

Before the bee, the woman hosting the event pieces together the top part of the quilt. To do this, she cuts and sews many small pieces of fabric to form a pattern. The Amish use a variety of quilt patterns and each pattern has its own name. Examples include Sunshine and Shadow, Tumbling Block, and Double Wedding Ring. Quilts are meant to be pleasing to the eye, so quilters take great care in selecting patterns and colors. Once the top is complete, it needs to be sewn to a layer of batting which provides insulation and texture. At the quilting bee, eight to sixteen women work together to stitch the top piece to a batting layer.

On the day of the quilting bee, women arrive at the host's home with preschool children in hand. The children play together and help thread needles while the women sit around a quilting frame, which stretches the material and holds it tight. This makes it easier for the women to stitch on the fabric. While the women sew, they talk about the weather, exchange recipes, and swap gardening tips. A writer who attended an Amish quilting bee notes that the lively conversation between the women appeared "more important than the stitching or production of a quilt."[61]

A Typical Day

A quilting bee offers a break from the normal routine, which begins before the sun comes up. At four or five o'clock in the morning, everyone rises to begin chores, which last between one and two hours. This excerpt from an Amish mother's diary describes a typical early morning:

> January 1: I was awake early to soak up the peace and solitude that only a mother can appreciate before her brood awakens. 4:30 A.M.—hubby and 16-year-old [son]

Josiah went to chore and milk 30 Holsteins. I went to the basement and did all the laundry early in the morning. Afterwards I went to the barn to wash the milkers and clean up the milk house. Also made my daily routine to the pig bar—a new litter of baby pigs greeted me. I do the teeth pinching and give shots, etc. with the new litter.[62]

Following chores, the entire family gathers at the breakfast table. There is a short, silent prayer before everyone starts to eat. Standard breakfast fare includes eggs, cornmeal mush, cereal, fried potatoes, canned fruit, and shoofly pie, a custard or soft gingerbread-like filling of molasses, sugar, butter, and flour baked in a pie crust. There is no small talk or chatting at the breakfast table. Instead, the father and mother discuss the work that needs to be done that day and who should do it. In some cases, parents assign children after-school chores.

When breakfast has ended, school-age children grab their lunches and head off to school. Depending on how far away the schoolhouse is, the children either walk or drive a cart. Older siblings, who have finished their education, spend the day working at home with their parents or at a nearby Amish-owned business. Boys help their fathers with farmwork while girls assist their mothers inside and around the house. The midday meal, which is called dinner, can be

Days begin early for the Amish, often before the sun comes up. Children and their parents complete many chores before breakfast.

eaten as early as eleven o'clock, and parents and children who have completed schooling eat dinner together. During this meal, young people provide progress reports on the jobs they are doing. Parents also update each other on events that have taken place so far in the day. Following the meal, everyone goes back to work.

When school-age children arrive home from school, they take a short snack break before starting their chores. In his book *Dust Between My Toes*, Wayne Weaver recalls the many chores and jobs he held while going to school. Weaver worked odd jobs at his father's feed mill and small dairy and poultry farm. He picked and sold strawberries, trapped muskrats, filled feedbags, and plowed the fields with a team of horses. In addition, both before and after school, Weaver and his siblings hand milked the family's herd of cows. Weaver's experience is the norm for Amish boys. Young girls, on the other hand, do more work around the home and help prepare meals and set the table.

Around four or five o'clock, the family gathers to eat supper. The Amish like rich, hearty foods, such as macaroni and cheese, meat loaf, dumplings, and desserts. There is little talk around the table. The only noise might be an occasional belch, which is considered a sign of a good appetite. After the mother and daughters clear the table and wash the dishes by hand, the family spends the evening in quiet activities.

For supper, the Amish enjoy rich foods like macaroni and cheese, dumplings, and meat loaf.

Playing Safety Games

Farms are not safe places, especially for young children. Potential hazards include getting hands caught in machinery or getting kicked by livestock. Since many Amish children help on the farm, a Pennsylvania organization created a board game that teaches farm safety to youngsters, according to a *Dallas Morning News* article entitled "Amish Children Encouraged to Play Games in the Name of Safety." The game allows players to move their playing piece ahead on the board after they have correctly answered a question about safe practices. The game has proven to be popular with Old Order Amish and Mennonite children.

"The thing is that Amish children love board games—Parcheesi, Monopoly, Candyland, Scrabble—probably more than your non-Amish kids do. They don't have video games to play with," said a woman who helped develop the game.

There has been one problem, however. Originally a nonprofit group had intended to give the games away free of charge. But Amish parents wouldn't agree to that and insisted upon paying. One of the game designers explained: "It was supposed to be free, but the people wouldn't accept that. . . . [This is a] community where they don't take anything for nothing."

Because of the absence of central heat and lighting systems, the family usually gathers in one room of the house, which typically contains a space heater. Parents like to read the local newspaper or a magazine. The Amish have publications of their own, including the *Budget*, a weekly newspaper, and *Family Life*, a magazine, but men also read *Popular Mechanics* and women enjoy cooking and sewing magazines. During this time, Amish children are free to read a book or play a board game as they have very little homework and are not expected to study at night. A visitor to an Amish school observes that when the children were dismissed to go home at three o'clock "hardly anyone carried a book home."[63] To the Amish, family togetherness is more important than book learning. Evenings are also an opportunity to sit and write letters to relatives who live far away. In addition, the mother might prepare a nighttime snack, such as homemade pretzels with lemonade or hot chocolate for everyone. At the end of the evening, the father leads the family in a short prayer before everyone goes to bed, usually around nine o'clock.

Visiting

Sundays, however, are considerably different. On the Sundays when there is no service, families can rest and relax. After morning chores, the family might gather around the table to study the German Bible or read Bible stories aloud.

Visiting is another Sunday activity that is central to the Amish culture. Families often spend the "off," or non-church, Sundays visiting friends or relatives. On these days, women prepare lunch for the entire group, which is followed by a leisurely afternoon of talking and eating snacks. In the tiny Amish community, visiting takes the place of non-Amish family outings such as spending the day at an amusement park. No invitation is necessary for families to visit relatives and, in fact, Sunday visiting is so common that most families expect guests to stop in during the day. Since the Amish don't have telephones, there's no way to call ahead and make plans. This means that a family might not be home when visitors drop by. When that

A family enjoys an outing in a closed carriage. Visiting on Sundays is a typical Amish activity.

happens, the visitors simply get back in their buggy and ride to the next farmhouse.

Holidays

Holidays are another time for visiting friends and relatives, and the Amish observe a number of special days including Christmas, Old Christmas (January 6, the date of Jesus' baptism), Good Friday, Easter, Ascension Day, Pentecost, and Thanksgiving. Christmas is the most important holiday but it doesn't include "worldly" customs such as decorated trees, Santa Claus, and festive parties. The Amish view these traditions as extravagant and unnecessary. In *Family Life*, a

mother explains why the Amish don't follow the custom of exchanging cards during the holiday season: "It's not necessary to send Christmas cards, for all our friends know we wish them well at Christmas and at other times of the year, too."[64]

Amish families do exchange gifts on December 25, however, but because they have such large families, it is too expensive to buy gifts for every family member. To solve the problem, family members draw a name and buy a gift only for that person. Typical presents for children include clothing, books, wooden animal toys, and homemade rag dolls. Older girls often receive household items, such as china, which they pack away in their hope chest for their own home and family.

Christmas dinners are elaborate meals, with food similar to that served at weddings. In addition to family gatherings, other groups get together for Christmas dinners, including single women, teachers, and parents. With so many gatherings, it can be difficult to accommodate everyone's schedule. As a result, the holiday season often extends well beyond December and early January; indeed, it is not uncommon to hold a Christmas dinner in February.

Recreation

Although this extended holiday season is a form of recreation, in general, there is very little emphasis on recreation in Amish life. The exception is an occasional family outing. Amish families don't go to movies, fairs, or concerts, however. Instead, they may eat at a restaurant or spend an afternoon at a zoo or museum.

By far, though, the most popular pastime is going to household or farm auctions. Teachers even let children leave school early on days when there is an auction. At farm auctions, farmers who are retiring or moving sell the equipment and animals they no longer need. As one observer notes: "The Amish loved going to auctions. Recycling household goods, farm machinery, or animals appealed to their practical nature. After a long day's work, a cattle auction was a chance to visit with friends and learn the latest cattle prices."[65]

Amish children also spend a great deal of time playing outdoors. Around the farm, they enjoy hayrides and riding ponies. In the winter,

Amish children spend a great deal of time outdoors. These boys ice-skate on a frozen pond.

they ice skate, sled, and have snowball fights. In the summer, camping, fishing, and ball games are popular as well as in-line skating. When writer Sue Bender stayed with an Amish family she encountered a group of children in the middle of a water fight. "It was a truly first-class, state-of-the-art water fight. There was no holding back . . . the children ran down to the barn, grabbed buckets, filled them with water from the cows' trough, and proceeded to drown each other in flying water."[66]

Farming

Although Amish children enjoy the occasional water fight, most of Amish life centers on operating small family farms. The Amish view the farm as the ideal place to live and raise a family. They value work and farms provide many opportunities for families to work together. The husband and older sons do the hard manual labor, and in the busy season, women and girls provide extra hands in the field.

Amish farms range from 80 to 150 acres in size, just what a man is capable of plowing, planting, and harvesting with a team of horses. On these farms, the Amish grow a variety of crops, including corn, oats, wheat, barley, hay, alfalfa, and clover. Most Amish farmers use pesticides to protect their crops, although certainly much less than their non-Amish peers, but a few Amish groups don't use any pesticides at all and grow food organically. Farmers also keep livestock, such as horses, cows, hogs, chickens, and sheep, and the milk from dairy cows provides a source of income.

Just as the *Ordnung* prohibits automobiles, it also prohibits certain modern farm practices, namely the use of tractors. A few groups do, however, allow members to have tractors with steel wheels because they believe that steel wheels are not as mobile as rubber tires and won't substantially change the way a farmer works in his fields. Most Amish farmers, though, rely completely on large, strong draft horses. Horses offer several advantages over tractors. Horse farmers can start plowing their fields earlier in the year. Furthermore, horses don't pack down the soil the way a tractor does. And horses provide free, natural fertilizer in the form of manure.

Stubborn as a Mule

Amish farmers generally keep six draft horses and two light horses for transportation, but some prefer to use mules. John Hostetler's book *Amish Roots: A Treasury of History, Wisdom, and Lore* includes the story of Gideon L. Fisher, an Amish farmer who was willing to give mules a try.

At an auction, Fisher purchased two mules, which he named Jewel and Dick. He planned to use the animals for plowing the following spring. The mules, he was informed, were not accustomed to humans. Consequently, Fisher "spent a lot of time that winter petting them, and trying to teach them that if they would respond, I would be a kind master." When spring came, Fisher discovered that Jewel was cooperative. But Dick was not. "When the harness touched his [Dick's] back he snorted and carried on, and did most anything to get out from under." Fisher finally managed to get Dick under control but experienced problems during plowing. "When I said, 'Whoa, Dick,' he did not stop . . . he didn't know what whoa meant. It seemed nothing would stop him." It took a while but eventually Dick changed. "With a lot of patience we got him to cooperate," says Fisher.

Most Amish farmers prefer to plow their fields with horses because the animals do not pack the soil and supply free fertilizer.

The Four Seasons

As on farms everywhere, Amish farm life follows the seasons. In spring, farmers plow the fields and plant seed. A farmer and three horses can plow one and a half to two acres a day. Spring is also the time to plant vegetables in the garden. Summer brings wheat and barley threshing. August offers downtime. Farmers are kept busy in September and October harvesting corn and digging up potatoes. And winter months are a good time to make repairs, mend harnesses, butcher animals, and trim apple trees.

One Task at a Time

Because there's a time and place for everything, the Amish don't see any value in hurrying. Whether they are quilting or plowing a field, the Amish never skip steps or rush to get a job over with quickly. This attention to detail is passed down from one generation to the next so that everyone knows what they are to do and how to do it.

When artist Sue Bender lived with an Amish family, she spent a day with a group of women who canned forty jars of peas. Bender was astonished that throughout the day-long process, the women took their time and focused on one task at a time. "No one rushed," writes Bender. "Each step was done with care. The women moved through the day unhurried. There was no rushing to finish so they could get on to the 'important things.' For them, it was all important."[67]

The Most Valuable Gift

Like these women, all Amish members work for the greater good of the family and community. Individuals don't seek fame and fortune through the work they do because work has another, more important, role. Through work, an individual shows concern and care for loved ones. Writer Wayne Weaver learned this lesson while growing up in an Amish community. When he was in sixth grade, he had the responsibility of making sure there

were plenty of dried corncobs in a small box next to the kitchen stove. Weaver's mother needed the corncobs to light the stove's fire, a task that had to be done every morning. One afternoon, Weaver forgot to bring the corncobs from the family's mill into the kitchen. At five o'clock the next morning, he says, "Mother wanted to kindle a fire and there were no corncobs. We slept upstairs where it got quite cold during the winter. I was roused out of bed onto the cold floor for a memorable trip through the dark to the mill for corncobs. A flashlight served for light. This only happened once and left me with a sense of what happens when people shirk their responsibility."[68]

Work and leisure activities, like everything else in the Amish culture, revolve around family life. The strength of the community is the strength of its families. But the Amish recognize that it takes time and effort to create these strong family bonds. In the Amish view, a family "needs to work together, visit friends together, read together, plan things together, eat together, share their joys and sorrow, hopes and disappointments. In short, the family needs to *live together*."[69]

CHAPTER 5

Our Own Schools

Until the mid–twentieth century, Amish children attended one-room public schools near their homes. But as rural schools began to consolidate in the 1940s and 1950s, Amish parents faced a difficult decision. They had to agree to send their children to large, more distant schools or defy state laws regarding compulsory education. Then, in 1972, the U.S. Supreme Court ruled that the Amish had the right to operate their own small, private schools. "In the years since the high court's decision," writes former Amish teacher Louise Stoltzfus, "these tiny institutions have become an integral part of the Amish landscape and community."[70]

The One-Room Schoolhouse

The schools that Amish children attend today resemble a school from the 1890s rather than a modern structure. The buildings have one or two classrooms that hold twenty to thirty students, or *scholars,* as the Amish call their schoolchildren, in grades one through eight. There also might be a bookroom and a basement, where children can play Ping-Pong or board games during recess and eat lunch when it is raining or cold outside.

Many of these schoolhouses are former public school buildings. As these small rural schools closed, Amish communities bought the

The Amish operate private one-room schools for their children.

buildings from the state and remodeled them so that they would reflect Amish beliefs. Sociologist John Hostetler notes that modifications included lowering high ceilings "to create a cozier, more homelike atmosphere."[71] Further, because Amish schools do not have electricity, schoolrooms lack electrical lights and computers. Instead, schools are designed to make the best use of natural light as possible. In areas where there is no indoor plumbing, students use outhouses, and outside hand pumps provide well water for drinking. Schools also have rope-pulled school bells, which the teacher or a student rings to signal the start of the school day and the end of recess and lunch.

The layout of Amish schools also provides places where the children can be creative and play. Hostetler describes some of these features: "Inside, colorful drawings and charts made by the [schoolchildren] may be found on walls and windows. Every schoolyard has a ball field. A few have swings or seesaws. Sledding and ice skating are considered when a site is located for a school."[72]

The Need for Amish Schools

Amish schools came about in response to changes in rural school systems that began after World War II. Before that, Amish children largely attended public schools. But over time, the one-room schoolhouses that served rural Amish communities proved a costly burden to state budgets. To save money, state boards of education began closing the rural schools and replacing them with large, consolidated schools. Because these schools were not nearby, children faced long bus rides, sometimes as long as an hour. The time spent on the bus meant that Amish children were unable to help with chores around the farm or home. The public schools also taught subjects that were contrary to Amish

values. As one Amish teacher explains to a non-Amish visitor: "We don't think we need all the science classes you have. We prefer Bible-based books. And we don't like gym classes where the children have to change clothes. We'd rather have plain old recess. And we don't agree with the way public schools have sex education."[73]

Additionally, non-Amish teachers often did not understand basic Amish beliefs, such

Amish girls play at recess. Amish schools are strict, but they also provide a place for the children to be creative and to play.

Amish schoolchildren are required to attend school only up to age fifteen, a rule that conflicted with state laws.

as lack of electricity or television. This lack of understanding caused problems between the two groups. For instance, one parent complained that a group of eighth-graders had been instructed to watch a television program at home. The next day, the students were tested on material from the program. Because the Amish students had not watched the show, they received failing marks on the test. Stories such as this convinced parents that public schools were too "worldly." One Amish writer wrote that public school education "teaches our children gross untruths about our origin and the Creation. It also exposes them to all kinds of vice and sin."[74]

Amish Beliefs Conflict with State Laws

Starting in the 1930s, rural school systems began raising the mandatory attendance age. Until then, Amish children had been required to go to school only until they were fourteen. But when school boards changed the minimum age to fifteen, children who had completed eighth grade but were not yet fifteen had to attend high school. This concerned Amish parents, who feared for their traditional way of life. As one Amishman writes, "For pity's sake, don't raise the school age for farm children . . . for if they don't do farm work while they're young they seldom care for it when they're older."[75]

In the decades that followed, Amish parents continued to clash with school boards over sending teenagers to high school. In some cases, parents simply had their children repeat eighth grade until the child turned fifteen. Other parents refused to send their children to school after the child finished eighth grade. In response, law enforcement officials fined and imprisoned Amish fathers who did not allow their fourteen-year-olds to attend school.

Since the Amish do not believe in using courts, the matter might never have been settled but for a group of people, led by a Lutheran minister, who went to court on behalf of the Amish. In the 1972 case *Wisconsin vs. Yoder*, the Supreme Court ruled in favor of the Amish.

Amish schools promote community ideals such as the strength of family, and discourage competition and pride.

The Court upheld the religious rights of the Amish, and ruled that Amish children did not have to attend high school. Despite this ruling, some states continue to harass Amish parents who do not allow their children to attend high school. But for the most part, the Amish are now free to educate their children in a way that is consistent with Amish values and way of life.

Their efforts have been successful. By the end of the 1990s, there were more than nine hundred Amish schools. There is no central body responsible for overseeing and maintaining these schools. Instead, each church district is responsible for managing the schools in its area, and parents pay tuition based on how many children they have attending the school.

An Amish Education

Another major difference between the Amish and public school systems is that the Amish school calendar is eight months long. This extended four-month summer vacation allows children to help their parents during planting and harvesting season. To make sure that students are in the classroom for the number of days required by law, Amish schools take a three-day Christmas break and very few other holidays off.

Further, in keeping with the spirit of *Gelassenheit*, Amish schools discourage ambition, competition, and pride. The book *The Amish School* explains the steps that an Amish community took to keep playground games from becoming too spirited:

> One school board has forbidden the use of baseball gloves and hard balls at school. By the children's playing with a sponge ball or other soft ball, and without gloves, baseball does not become a competitive game with "worldly" methods which might range out of control among teenagers and be carried on into adulthood.[76]

Preventing such competitive play, the Amish contend, affirms their society's belief in the value of all members and the idea that everyone has something to offer. To instill this concept in young people, teachers encourage students to achieve to their personal best and not to rate themselves against their classmates. As one former Amish teacher writes: "At some time or another, children need to learn to work without being rewarded, to learn that achievement in itself is reward. . . . A goal each pupil can work for is to make a higher score than he did the day before."[77]

The purpose of Amish schools is to prepare children to be productive members of their community. Amish teachers emphasize neatness, especially when it comes to penmanship. Legible handwriting is important in the Amish community, which relies heavily on written communication. The lack of electronic equipment, such as computers, means that invitations, announcements, and letters must all be handwritten. Amish schools also stress discipline and adherence to community rules. For instance, boys are required to wear their hats whenever they are outside, and an Amish teacher recalls that she would remind boys "to wear their hats on the playground and keep their shirt collars buttoned in the schoolroom."[78]

Additionally, Amish children are taught practical skills they will need to manage a home or farm. For instance, students study mathematics in such applications as measuring baking ingredients or keeping track of farm income and expenses. According to a former schoolteacher, a successful Amish education is one where students learn "how to borrow and lend money, how to sew their own clothes, plan and cook meals, prepare a field, and drive a horse and buggy team."[79]

A Two-Part System

An Amish education is divided into two parts. The first part is the elementary school curriculum, which is conducted in one- or two-room schoolhouses and lasts through the eighth grade. The Amish believe that an elementary education is enough formal academic preparation for life as a farmer or homemaker. They think that it is more useful for teenagers to work than to go to school. An Amish writer explained the Amish view of education: "Among all the Amish people in Lancaster County, you couldn't find one who ever took any high school, college, or vocational school education. Yet I don't believe there's a class of people in the entire world that lead a happier life than do our people."[80]

It's Off to School We Go

In his book *Driving the Amish*, Jim Butterfield describes the scene on the road early in the morning as Amish children make their way to school.

We passed some boys walking the gravel roads, carrying lunch buckets, and wearing black hats. Farther on, a group of young girls wore bonnets, and some carried black umbrellas because it was raining a bit. Every three or four miles on this fall morning, we passed other small schoolhouses with lazy smoke coming from their chimneys.

Near the edge of a woods, we saw Hickory Grove [an Amish school] and heard the first bell at eight o'clock as we drove in. The school, fairly new, is built of cement blocks with a wooden shed behind for horses. Most of the children walk, but a few come almost three miles and use carts or a small covered spring wagon.

Have Bookmobile, Will Travel

For Amish schoolchildren, getting to a public library can be difficult. The Amish don't have cars and children are kept busy with farm chores. But a twenty-eight-foot book-

mobile helps make sure that the six thousand Amish children and adults in rural Geauga County, Ohio, can keep up with their reading. In a *Washington Times* article entitled "Taking Books to TV-free Territory . . ." Amy Sancetta reports that the bookmobile, which is part of the county public library system, stops in Amish communities three of its six weekly days of operation.

Children walk for a mile to return books and check out new ones. According to a bookmobile librarian, the Amish like to read westerns, Hardy Boys mysteries, and inspirational books. The Amish community appreciates the efforts of the bookmobile staff. "The Amish do love us," a librarian said. "They let us use their outhouses. They bring us fresh bakery. And at Christmas, they bring us something at every stop—bread and baked goods and deer jerky."

Because getting to the library is difficult for Amish children, many take advantage of bookmobiles offered in their areas.

The second stage of education is a vocational training program for students who have completed eighth grade but who still are required by law to be in school. As part of the program, students receive a few hours of instruction every week and spend the remainder of the time learning farming or homemaking from their parents.

Fund-Raising

With their own school system firmly in place, Amish communities must work to keep the schools going. Operating and maintaining an

Amish school is a group effort. Every year, Amish parents hold auctions to raise money for schools and members of the community donate items to be sold. One such event is the All Wisconsin Draft Horse, Machinery, and Quilt Consignment Auction, held in Albany, Wisconsin. The highlight of the auction is the colorful handmade Amish quilts offered for sale. Women from settlements throughout the Midwest and as far away as Pennsylvania and New York contribute quilted bedspreads and wall hangings. About three to four hundred quilt pieces are auctioned each year, some receiving bids as high as a thousand dollars. Other items are sold as well, including farm machinery and furniture. This money supplements the tuition paid by parents and is used to buy textbooks and to pay teachers.

School Boards

In addition to fund-raising, community members serve on the school board, which oversees hiring teachers and buying books and materials. School boards look for textbook and reference materials that conform to Amish standards. They object to content about computers or sex education, or which contradicts their religion, such as the teaching of evolution. Thus, school boards often buy old books that other schools have discarded and as a result, many Amish students use outdated textbooks. One visitor to an Amish school in the 1990s made the following observation about the percentage problems the students were working on:

> Eighth grade had to figure out Charles Lindbergh's average speed across the Atlantic if he flew 3,647 miles in 33.5 hours. In fact, one whole page of their *Strayer-Upton Practical Arithmetic* was devoted to problems about Lindbergh and the *Spirit of St. Louis*. I turned to the title page and, sure enough, the copyright date was 1928, one year after his [Lindbergh's] famous flight!"[81]

Recently, however, a growing number of publishing companies have begun to specialize in producing textbooks for Amish schools. One such company is Pathway Publishers in Aylmer, Ontario. Pathway publishes a series of readers for grades one through eight that include illustrations of subjects familiar to Amish children such as horses and buggies, farm animals, and wood-burning stoves. Like Pathway, another publisher, Gordonville Print Shop, based in Gordonville, Pennsylvania, publishes mathematics textbooks geared to the needs of a one-room classroom. Both Pathway and Gordonville books also offer workbooks that make it easy for students to study on their own and require only minimum guidance from the teacher. In addition to their textbooks, Amish children read approved non-Amish classic literature, such as *Little Women* by Louisa May Alcott.

Parental Involvement

In addition to fund-raising, parents play other important roles in the operating of their community's school. They help to repair and clean the school building, for instance. Every fall a few

Amish parents are very involved in their children's education.

weeks before school begins, a day is set aside to paint and fix up the school. During the summer recess, parents mow the lawn; during the school term, they make certain there is enough firewood and coal on hand to burn in the furnace.

Parents get involved in other, more fun, ways, too, such as hosting a School Singing. Students and parents gather at the host family's house in the evening to sing songs and enjoy treats like lemonade, soft pretzels, sugar cookies, and homemade root beer.

Sometimes a family hosts lunch, as happened one afternoon to an Amish teacher and her students. The teacher recalls:

> I had planned to have the children walk in pairs to this couple's home (even the children of that household did not know about it [the lunch]), but then I was surprised when I looked out the window and saw the father with a two-horse wagon and bales of straw for seats, ready to transport us to their home.

> When we got there, we found a long table laden with a delicious hot meal. After eating, we spent a half hour playing at the farm before the father gave us a wagon ride back to school.[82]

Christmas Programs and Summer Picnics

Organized school activities such as Christmas programs also bring families, teachers, and students together. Not every Amish school offers a Christmas program, but in those that do it is a much-anticipated event. A typical program might include poems, plays, and singing carols. Like the rest of Amish life, these Christmas programs are family and community affairs. One teacher describes how parents helped prepare for the school's pageant:

> Fathers spent part of a Saturday constructing a stage. Mothers agreed to help with simple costumes for Mary and Joseph, wise men and shepherds. On the scheduled evening, the entire local Amish community streamed into the gas-lit schoolroom, brimming with excitement and energy."[83]

In addition, school picnics, held at the end of the school term, give parents a chance to get together and talk while their children play lawn games. Sometimes the adults join in the games, which can include volleyball or softball. For lunch, mothers bring an assortment of food ranging from casseroles to chocolate cakes. An eighth-grade Amish girl recalls a last day of school picnic: "Everyone brought something along to eat and after lunch, the teacher . . . made a speech, and then us eighth graders were asked to come up front and were given our graduation gifts, a plate with our name, date, and the school name on it. After that we played a game of baseball, scholars [schoolchildren] vs. the fathers."[84]

Teacher Training

To educate their youngsters, the Amish need teachers who subscribe to the culture's unique way of life. Most Amish teachers are unmarried women who have not completed school beyond the eighth grade. Although a few teachers do take extension classes or correspondence courses, additional schooling is not necessary to become a teacher. Instead, school boards look for qualities such as a deep religious faith, interest in teaching, and an ability to handle children.

Teachers in the Amish community are often unmarried women who have no education beyond the eighth grade.

In general, Amish teachers learn by watching more experienced teachers and attending teachers' conferences. At the conferences, teachers exchange ideas and offer each other advice. A magazine, called *Blackboard Bulletin*, also offers tips on teaching. One Amish teacher explains the advice he took from the magazine: "It gave me the nerve to spank a boy who wouldn't stop pestering other scholars. He always found some way to push their papers or jiggle their desks. I was afraid to punish him till the *Blackboard Bulletin* said that sometimes a spanking is due—as long as there is love behind it." [85]

Although Amish teachers can spank a child to maintain discipline, such action is not

In the Amish community, student-teacher relationships resemble family relationships.

common, and Amish classrooms usually run smoothly. Schoolchildren are expected to behave and to show respect for the teacher. Even so, the student-teacher relationship is more like that of family members, with the teacher acting as a parent or older brother or sister. According to one Amish student who had previously attended a public school, "I'm sure I would never want to go back to the public school. This [Amish] school is much more like a big casual sort of family." [86] Both students

and teachers address each other by first name, and on holidays and special occasions they exchange gifts.

A Typical School Day

Holidays and special occasions provide a chance to play and rest, but most of the time students follow a strict daily schedule that starts at 8:30 A.M. The teacher arrives an hour earlier and writes the day's assignments on the blackboard. After the school bell has been rung, the students take their seats, usually sitting near others who are in the same grade. On average, there are three to five students in each grade.

Before they start any lessons, the teacher reads a short passage from the Bible. Then the students recite the Lord's Prayer before standing and going to the front of the room to sing a few songs. Jim Butterfield visited an Amish school, called Hickory Grove, where he noted the lyrics to one of the songs that the children sang:

> We're the crew of Hickory Grove,
>   A very lively set.
> We learn the lesson in our books
>   And hope we don't forget.
>
> Our schoolroom is a happy place;
>   We're not allowed to fight.
> Just smile and say good morning,
>   To start the day off right.[87]

After the morning song, the students return to their seats and begin their lessons. Throughout the day, the teacher takes turns reviewing subjects with each grade while the other students work quietly at their desks. Morning classes include reading, arithmetic, history, and geography.

Because a teacher is responsible for eight grades, she is constantly busy and must assign students to work independently. Early in the morning, the older students work on math assignments while the first graders practice English vocabulary with the teacher. The teacher then instructs the first graders to practice writing those new words while she turns her attention to the second graders. After the teacher works with the second graders, she reviews the work of the third graders. Following that, she works with the fourth, fifth, and sixth

graders. During this time, the seventh and eighth graders work in pairs or in a group to complete geography or history assignments. Sometimes the teacher will also ask an older student to lend a hand by listening to the younger children read or grading papers. An Amish student who had previously attended a public school, made this entry in her diary a month after she started attending an Amish school: "We have now learned to concentrate better when other grades are having their classes, but I'm sure it takes a lot of good management on the teacher's part to keep all these grades busy."[88]

At 10:00, there is a fifteen-minute recess, and then classroom instruction continues until lunch break at 11:30. At recess and lunch children can play outside or stay inside and shoot darts or play board games. At 12:30, the students return to their seats for a fifteen-minute story time. During the afternoon, students study such subjects as health, grammar, and spelling. One day a week, the students study High German. School ends at 3:00 P.M.

Special Education

In general children with handicaps attend the local one-room school and study alongside their classmates. In some cases, however, children with special needs or conditions such as deafness and Down's syndrome go to state-operated classes, where they receive specialized care. In Lancaster County, Pennsylvania, however, there are two Amish schools for children with special needs. Although the teachers in these schools don't receive any specific training, they do offer the children individualized attention, and students in these schools can take frequent breaks. Even so, the classroom remains orderly and quiet.

What's for Lunch?

There are no cafeterias in Amish schools; pupils bring sack lunches. In warm weather, a typical lunch might include a sandwich, celery, a piece of fruit, and milk. During the colder months, Amish schoolchildren can use their noses as well as the clock on the wall to know when it's time for lunch. In this excerpt from *The Amish School* by Sara E. Fisher and Rachel K. Stahl, a former Amish schoolteacher explains how the classroom sometimes doubles as a kitchen.

In the wintertime the teacher tries to arrive at school about an hour before school starts to fire up the stove and have the schoolroom warm and cozy when children arrive. . . .

Sometimes children bring potatoes wrapped in aluminum foil to roast on the ledge inside the top furnace door. Or they may bring a TV-dinner made from leftovers from their meal the night before, placed in a pie plate that can be heated on the stove for lunch. Some bring soup in a glass jar to put on the grate to heat. Others have sandwiches, hot dogs, or pizza to warm on the stove. All kinds of delicious smells fill the schoolroom as lunchtime nears.

Amish children eat their lunches at school.

One Amish teacher, who visited a special school, learned that the students enjoyed helping out in their classroom as much as her own students did. At the start of the school day, she saw several children fill their cups with water at the faucet. "There was no drainpipe and the overflow from their cups ran into a plastic bucket set underneath the sink. Since this schoolroom is located in the basement of a schoolhouse, and there is no electric pump to pump out the drain, the children covet the responsibility of emptying the bucket when it gets full." [89]

Both special and regular schools work hand in hand with parents to help all the children in the community become, as one writer puts it, "useful, God-fearing, law-abiding citizens." [90] In addition to teaching basic reading and writing skills, Amish schools stress the importance of Amish virtues. In this way, the schools prepare children to live a plain life independent of the modern world.

Interaction with *Englishers*

Although the Amish strive for self-sufficiency, they still must rely on the outside world and such institutions as hospitals, banks, and law enforcement for a variety of services. Their goal, therefore, is to limit contact with the outside world rather than eliminate it. But as farmland disappears and tourists clog rural highways, the Amish face more interaction with outsiders, or *Englishers*, not less. Thus, the Amish must find a balance between their need to be separate from the world and their increasing dependence on it.

Love Thy Enemy

For the most part, the Amish are peaceful, law-abiding citizens. Sometimes, however, state or federal laws go against the basic tenets of the Amish faith. When that happens, the Amish don't obey the law because they won't concede or compromise their religious principles. As a result, over the years, Amish beliefs have clashed with the U.S. government. One major conflict was over Amish children attending high school. Another major conflict centered on mandatory military service for Amish men.

The Amish are pacifists. They believe it is wrong to take another person's life, even in self-defense. The Amish firmly believe in the Bible's command to "love thy enemy" and, therefore, will not serve in the military or help raise funds for the armed services.

This stand put the Amish at odds with the federal government in 1917, when the United States entered World War I. At the time, the federal government was selling bonds to support the overseas war effort. Local officials urged the Amish to buy the war bonds. When the Amish refused to support any war effort, their loyalty to the United States was questioned. A citizen who didn't buy bonds was sometimes called a traitor, or friend of the enemy. In addition to name calling, Amish churches were vandalized. In a few cases, Amish citizens bought bonds just to keep the peace—although doing so went against their beliefs.

Combat Duty

In November 1917, when the United States entered World War I, the government drafted Amish young men into the military. The Amish agreed to go into the service but did so only as religious conscientious objectors (COs). COs are allowed to fulfill their military duty without having to fight in the war. Although the army did allow and make room for conscientious objectors, it was unclear what type of duty they would perform. Unable to find a quick solution, the government sent COs, including the Amish, to military training camps. At camp, other draftees and officers pressured the Amish to take up rifles. In some cases, the harassment worked and Amish men joined the fighting corps. Many held out, though, refusing to carry a weapon or wear a uniform. As one writer puts it, "Most of the brethren [Amish] proved stead fast in the faith and would have been willing to face the firing squad rather than go against their convictions."[91] Those Amish who refused endured beatings and verbal abuse. Some were even jailed until the war ended.

Alternative Service

Twenty years later, during World War II, the situation had changed. COs were not sent to military training camps. Instead, they were permitted to work at jobs that served the public good. Amish churches also got involved and funded these work camps, which assigned Amish men to fight forest fires and study farming methods.

When that war ended, the U.S. government established the 1-W program, which permitted conscientious objectors alternative service working in mental hospitals. This program actually caused many problems for the Amish as young men often spent their 1-W service living in big cities far away from their hometowns. This made it difficult for parents to communicate easily with their sons. In addition, the young men began to change as they adapted to the new environment where they lived. They

As an alternative to military service, draft-age Amish men may serve the public good in 1-W programs established by the U.S. government.

stopped wearing traditional Amish clothes, purchased cars, and dated non-Amish girls. When their service ended, many found it difficult to return to the small Amish communities where they had grown up. In 1969, the government responded to Amish requests and changed the 1-W program to allow Amish men to work on privately owned farms for a two-year period.

House Passes Amish Labor Law

Like their strong religious beliefs, work is vital to Amish culture and, while most American teens spend their day in the classroom, Amish teens spend their day working. After completing the eighth grade, Amish teenagers spend the next few years learning a trade or skill as apprentices. Traditionally, teenage boys worked with their father on the family farm. But as farmland becomes increasingly scarce, many Amish are opening small family businesses, such as woodworking mills. These mills provide jobs for teenage boys, who work alongside parents and relatives.

This situation bothers officials at the Department of Labor, the federal cabinet department that oversees workplace safety and enforces child labor laws. Many people there worry that the mill jobs endanger Amish teenagers. The labor secretary wrote, "Injury data collected over several decades consistently show that the lumber and wood products industry is particularly hazardous for adults, let alone children."[92]

As a result of these concerns, the Labor Department instituted strict guidelines as to when and where the children could work. These guidelines included a law that prohibited children under fifteen from holding jobs in woodworking mills. Based on that law, the Department of Labor fined Amish parents who employed their sons at the mills.

In the late 1990s, however, the Amish went to Washington, D.C., and asked the

High Court Ruling

Throughout the 1960s Amish parents and school boards clashed over the issue of Amish teenagers attending high school. In the end, a 1972 U.S. Supreme Court decision resolved the dispute in favor of the Amish. The book *A History of the Amish* by Steven M. Nolt includes the ruling of Chief Justice Warren Burger, who wrote the following majority opinion for the Court:

Amish objection to formal education beyond the eighth grade is firmly ground in . . . central religious concepts. They object to high school and higher education generally because the values it teaches are in marked variance with Amish values and the Amish way of life. . . . The high school tends to emphasize intellectual and scientific accomplishments, self-determination, competitiveness, worldly success, and social life with other students. Amish society emphasizes learning-through-doing, a life of "goodness," rather than a life of intellect, wisdom, rather than technical knowledge, community welfare rather than competition, and separation rather than integration with contemporary worldly society.

. . . There can be no assumption that today's majority is "right" and the Amish and others like them are "wrong." A way of life that is odd or even erratic but interferes with no rights or interests of others is not to be condemned because it is different.

House of Representatives to pass special legislation permitting Amish youth to work in the mills under the watchful eye of an adult. Amish parents told lawmakers that safety is important to them also and that they take precautions to protect underage workers. Parents explained that the Department of Labor's restrictions threatened the Amish way of life because children were not able to learn and work alongside their parents and relatives. As a result, in March 1999 the House of Representatives passed a law allowing Amish teens to work in woodworking mills. The government still imposed some restrictions, however. The teens can only do jobs around the mill such as writing orders, sweeping, and stacking wood, and they must follow strict safety procedures and cannot operate machinery.

Although the new law passed unanimously, some officials are still worried. They believe the mills are a dangerous environment for young people. "Adult presence in the workplace cannot protect children from the split-second mistake that could cost them a finger, hand or worse,"[93] writes one government representative.

Youth Problems

The way Amish youth spend their time does not exclude social problems found outside Amish society. In 1998, the *Dallas Morning News* ran the headline, "Amish Drug Problems."[94] The article reported that two Pennsylvania men had been arrested and charged with selling cocaine to a youth gang. Although the story was alarming it wasn't unusual, and the article probably would not have been picked up by newspapers around the country except for the fact that the two men were Amish and the gang was an Amish youth gang.

Many outsiders think that peaceful, rural Amish communities are immune to problems such as drinking, illegal drug use, or teenage violence. But they aren't. These types of behavior happen far less among the Amish, but they do happen. Young men form social gangs with names such as Kirkwooders, Shotguns, Pioneers, and Luckies. Members of these gangs meet on weekend nights and drink alcohol. In Hazleton, Iowa, for example, forty Amish teenage boys who had been drinking went on a rampage and vandalized a local family's property. According to a neighbor, "Drinking up here has been going on for years. These kids' parents and grandparents did it. They didn't raise hell like this bunch, but it's nothing new."[95]

Drinking and Driving a Buggy

The Amish problem of underage drinking causes problems for more than just the Amish themselves. On Saturday nights in Geauga County, Ohio, for instance, hundreds of Amish teens gather at bonfire parties where they drink beer. In recent years there have been serious incidents involving intoxicated Amish youth. In one case, a teen who had been drinking beer passed out in his buggy. This left his horse to trot unguided alongside traffic and through busy intersections. A local police chief said the situation was alarming: "The horse doesn't know when to stop for signs. It was a recipe for disaster."[96]

In responce to such concerns, county authorities are working to solve the problem by offering a variety of outreach programs. A few years ago, the Geauga County sheriff spoke to a gathering of sixteen hundred Amish adults and teens about the dangers of alcohol. In addition, a juvenile judge sends fifty Amish youngsters a year to Turning Point, an alcohol awareness class. The county's nearly forty

Community members who are harassed or abused are often reluctant to seek justice because the Amish are a passive, self-reliant people.

Amish schools also participate in the Drug Abuse Resistance Education (DARE) program, which teaches students the dangers of drugs and alcohol and how to withstand peer pressure to drink.

Turn the Other Cheek

Not all the Amish's problems are alcohol related. In fact, the very qualities for which they are known—nonassertiveness, self-reliance,

nonresistance—sometimes make them targets for vandals. In 1997 a small Amish community in Wisconsin finally admitted to authorities that three men had been harassing residents for a year. The vandals had been throwing bottles, rocks, and bricks at Amish buggies and had stolen a buggy and burned it. A law enforcement official speculated why the three men acted the way they did. He said, "It may be because these people pick on people who they know are not going to fight back, whose philosophy is to turn the other cheek."[97] The Amish are normally reluctant to notify authorities, but after the buggy-burning incident they promised to report any vandalism or harassment.

Genetic Research

One aspect of the outside world that the Amish have been willing to participate in, however, is scientific research on genetic diseases. Because the Amish are such an insulated society, they have a high rate of inherited disorders, such as dwarfism, hemophilia, and liver disease. To help find cures for inherited diseases, Amish parents have been willing to let researchers conduct ongoing studies of Amish children afflicted with genetic disorders.

Two scientists from the eastern United States, Dr. Jerod Lucey from the University of Vermont and Dr. Attallah Kappas of Rockefeller University, are working to help Amish children who suffer from Crigler-Najjar syndrome, a liver disease that can be fatal. The two make visits to Lancaster County, Pennsylvania, to speak to families who have children with Crigler-Najjar. There are three hundred cases of Crigler-Najjar in the world and sixteen are found in the Pennsylvania Amish community. Children who have Crigler-Najjar must spend up to sixteen hours a day under special lights that help break down a substance in their bodies that can cause severe brain damage. In some cases, Amish families put generators in the children's rooms to operate the lights but still use old-fashioned lamps throughout the rest of the house.

Amish families welcome this help from the outside world. An Amish father, who attended a two-day meeting with Drs. Lucey and Kappas, said, "I want to see what we can learn here. Maybe together we can come up with new ways to cure this thing." [98]

Tobacco

Besides genetic disorders, the Amish face other health problems. And some of these concerns have even gone so far as to create a major controversy within the church. At the center of the controversy is whether the Amish should be allowed to smoke cigarettes. Certain church districts see nothing wrong with the men in their community smoking cigarettes. But other congregations disapprove of tobacco use, believing that because it has harmful effects on the body, it goes against church values. The writer of a letter that appeared in *Family Life* magazine pleads for all Amish to stop smoking cigarettes: "It's time to face the facts and realize that using tobacco is a lust of the flesh, a harm to your health, and a waste of your money." [99]

Just as smoking tobacco is controversial, Amish farmers' growing tobacco as a cash crop

Growing tobacco has created controversy for the Amish, but it remains an ideal crop because it can be grown on small-acreage farms.

causes conflict among the various Amish groups. Many Amish feel it is wrong to make money from a product that causes harm to people. But other groups, who have long relied on the income from tobacco, believe there is nothing wrong with harvesting the crop.

Tobacco is a labor-intensive crop that can be grown on small-acreage farms, and as such is an ideal crop for Amish farmers. Thus, the controversy presents a quandary for the farmers. Although they, for the most part, agree that growing tobacco is detrimental to their communities, they are financially dependent on the crop. According to one tobacco farmer, "We heartily agree to all you [those who oppose growing tobacco] have said, but what can we do? We grow the stuff. It's like this: we live on a small farm in Lancaster County, and I'm sure you know the price of land here. We have no dairy nor money to put one in. . . . Shall we buy another farm? Where? With what? . . . What can we do?"[100]

A Changing Landscape

Although the Amish have a long history of working as farmers, controversy over planting tobacco and other problems are increasingly forcing them to seek out other occupations. In the 1950s, 95 percent earned a living as farmers. By 1996 that number had decreased to 50 percent. A main reason for the change is that there simply isn't enough good land available for all the young people who want to own a farm. This is especially true in older, more crowded settlements in Pennsylvania, Ohio, and Indiana.

Traditionally, Amish parents have helped their children buy a farm. But with cost of farmland skyrocketing, even pooling funds for land purchase has become difficult. In Pennsylvania, for instance, a hundred-acre farm can cost one million dollars or more, and the Amish must also compete against well-funded developers who buy the land so they can build new houses or shopping malls, not farms. Developers win about 50 percent of the time. In Lancaster County a developer recently turned former farmland into a miniature golf course. The course is right next to a seventy-five-acre Amish dairy farm. "I don't think it's being a good steward of the land," the farmer said of the golf course development. "One thing about farming ground, once it is used for something else, it will never be returned to farm ground."[101] Some Amish have pulled up stakes and moved to less congested areas of the country. But not everyone wants to move, and those who stay must find work besides farming.

The Next Best Thing

For the Amish, the best alternative to farming is a home-based business. These businesses, which are located in a separate building on the farm, include bakeries, bicycle sales and service shops, wool mills, and quilt shops. There are few employees, mostly family members. Both men and women operate home businesses, which often supplement farm income. Although Amish men traditionally earned the money while women took care of the home, the fact that women are now helping with the finances doesn't seem to be a problem. One Amish wife and mother who runs a home quilting business explains why:

> Often the quilt money is needed promptly to help make one payment or another. My husband is grateful to me whenever I sign that quilt check and hand it to him. . . . As I think of hours I labored and the fingers I pricked until they bled, I feel it is a great reward when the quilt is sold and another debt can be paid.[102]

Amish home-based businesses like this carriage shop supplement farm income.

Tourism

In many cases, Amish home-based businesses capitalize on the tourist boom to Amish areas. Lancaster County, Pennsylvania, the oldest settlement, receives 4 million visitors a year. Holmes County, Ohio, home to the largest Amish settlement, accommodates almost 3 million tourists a year. Many of these visitors come to buy Amish-made goods because the quality of Amish products is widely respected. One Amish family in Pennsylvania sells homemade towels, potholders,

Amish-made food products are popular with tourists and are also an important income for the Amish.

and cookbooks, and Amish women also make homemade noodles, jams, and quilts to sell to tourists.

But tourists also cause problems for the Amish. Visitors often don't understand Amish culture or respect Amish ways. One Amishman had these comments about tourists: "They invade your privacy. They are a nuisance when I go to town, for I can't go to any public place without being confronted by tourists who ask dumb questions and take pictures."[103] However, even though tourists cause disruptions, they also bring in much-needed dollars to the Amish community. As a repre-

sentative of the Ohio Amish noted, "The fact is that you can hardly bite the hand that feeds you. The Amish just could not continue living in this community if they didn't have the possibility of crafts, because farmland is just sold out."[104]

Lean-and-Mean Business Machine

Despite the tourism concerns, the Amish, for the most part, have proved themselves capable entrepreneurs. Today, more than one thousand

Amish businesses operate with a failure rate of less than 5 percent, an impressive success rate compared with the nearly 75 percent of non-Amish businesses that fail. A sociologist notes that the Amish are succeeding, even though they don't have "strategic plans, marketing plans, telephones, computers, electricity, automobiles."[105] And according to one scholar, Amish businesses are doing well because they are "a no-frills, lean-and-mean kind of approach. No high-tech, no carpets."[106]

Although Amish businesses are low tech, they still need to advertise their goods and services. For many years, Amish-owned stores have placed ads in magazines but now some businesses are taking the next step and marketing their goods online. The owners are optimistic that the Internet can increase their sales. Since the Amish are forbidden to use computers, another company sets up the website and takes the orders. About eight Amish businesses have signed up for this service.

Home-based businesses are having another effect on the Amish way of life. Traditionally, the Amish have not allowed telephones inside their homes. Instead, they had telephone shanties, which were found at the end of a farm lane or outside a barn or shed. These small telephone booths allowed Amish families to make outgoing telephone calls. But, increasingly, the Amish are installing phones in their homes. The phones are to be used for business purposes only, but an

Home-based businesses and the Amish people who run them are changing the rules in many communities. For example, some groups even allow telephones inside members' homes.

occasional chat about the weather is not taboo. Small business owners say the telephone is essential to running their business and some even have voice mail. "It gets to the point that we can't do business without it," one Amish businessman says of the telephone. "And our church leaders realize this, and that's why they're letting it come in."[107]

"My Brain Just Went Dead Feeding Chickens"

Some Amish welcome the chance to work outside the farm. Moses Smucker, an Amish businessman, decided not to take over the family farm after his father's death. Smucker says he didn't like farmwork: "My brain just went dead feeding chickens and milking cows. I just kept thinking: 'There has to be more to life than driving down the field and coming back again.'"[108] After turning his back on farming, Smucker opened a leatherworking shop in 1971. Today

that shop sells harnesses, leather goods, and sleighs. Smucker supplies goods for many well-known animals, including the Budweiser Clydesdale horses and the pets of celebrities; Michael Jackson is one of his clients.

Smucker's leatherworking shop falls into a category of Amish-owned businesses that manufacture or make goods supporting the Amish lifestyle, such as buggy making, furniture making, and farm-equipment manufacturing. These businesses tend to be larger than the home-based businesses, generally are operated away from the farm, and require employees to commute. By all accounts Smucker is doing well financially. But more important to him is the fact that he runs his business within the guidelines of the *Ordnung*. He employs fewer than twenty-five workers and uses generators to operate sewing machines, rivet guns, and leather trimmers. He also has non-Amish employees drive him whenever he must make a business trip that is too far away to go by horse and buggy.

Hollywood Comes to the Amish

To the Amish, filmmaking, perhaps more than any other industry, symbolizes the corrupt outside world. For this reason, the Amish don't watch movies. But the fact that the Amish strongly oppose motion pictures hasn't stopped Hollywood from producing feature films using Amish characters. One such film, *Witness*, which was filmed in Lancaster, Pennsylvania, in1984, caused a flurry of protest from local Amish residents. The drama starred Harrison Ford as a police officer and Kelly McGillis as a young Amish widow, and depicted a violent gunfight on an Amish homestead. In the book *The Riddle of Amish Culture*, sociologist Donald B. Kraybill explains that the Amish felt they were being exploited and unfairly depicted. Amish bishops even warned members not to cooperate with the movie production crew. "We can't stop them," said an Amishman, "but we don't have to help them." The Amish took their complaints to the governor of Pennsylvania and a settlement was struck between the state and Amish leaders. In the settlement, the state agreed to inform potential producers of the Amish community's objections to being represented in a film. In addition, the state promised to stop promoting the Amish as subjects for feature films and dealing with companies that trespassed on Amish property.

Some Amish welcome the opportunity to work outside the home. These women cheerfully serve customers at a farmers' market.

The Lunch-Pail Problem

In addition to opening their own businesses, the lack of farmland forces Amish men to find other forms of employment. In some cases, Amish men work in nearby factories but these jobs can cause problems for the Amish workers, who come from a culture that emphasizes accuracy rather than speed. The workers become frustrated when their non-Amish employers expect them to do a task quickly, as doing things in a hurry is not the Amish way. An Amishman who left factory work had this to say about his former employment: "When I worked in the factory I was always pushed to work faster. I'd rather work slowly and see things are done right."[109] Another worker said of his nearly twenty years of factory work: "In factory life the more you do, the more they want you to do."[110]

In addition to factory work, many Amishmen hire themselves out as carpenters on construction crews. This causes problems, however, as the men are picked up and driven to work sites that are sometimes far from home. Such commutes mean that the men are gone all day from their homes and families. The Amish call this situation the lunch-pail problem, referring to the fact that the men carry a lunch with them rather than eat lunch at home with the family.

Some Amish fathers, however, have found a way to balance offsite work with their family life. Says one Amish worker:

I think the man's personal attitude toward his work and his family makes a big difference and determines whether there is a lunch-pail problem. Those who work away from home need to gear their life so they will have several special hours a day together with the family. It can be done. I feel I have seen cases where the busy young farmer did not succeed as well as the happy factory worker or carpenter.[111]

For now, happy or not with their outside jobs, the Amish are managing to keep interactions with the rest of the world to a minimum. It is uncertain, though, how long they can continue to do this. As Amish goods and services become more sought after by outsiders, it seems likely that the two cultures will interact more. When this happens, it's possible that the Amish will have to adapt and modify their lifestyle to accommodate the majority, for as one Amish writer notes, "The truth is that the wolf of worldliness is at our door and ready to devour the sheep."[112]

Notes

Introduction: An Inherited Way of Life

1. Quoted in Brad Igou, comp., *The Amish in Their Own Words: Amish Writings from 25 Years of* Family Life *Magazine*. Scottdale, PA: Herald Press, 1999, pp. 61–62.
2. Sue Bender, *Plain and Simple: A Woman's Journey to the Amish*. New York: Harper-Collins, 1989, pp. 50–51.

Chapter 1: "A Sacred Trust"

3. Quoted in Donald B. Kraybill, *The Riddle of Amish Culture*. Baltimore: Johns Hopkins University Press, 1991, p. 42.
4. John A. Hostetler, *Amish Society*. 4th ed. Baltimore: Johns Hopkins University Press, 1993, pp. 237–38.
5. Hostetler, *Amish Society*, p. 111.
6. Kraybill, *The Riddle of Amish Culture*, p. 35.
7. Kraybill, *The Riddle of Amish Culture*, p. 29.
8. Quoted in Kraybill, *The Riddle of Amish Culture*, p. 30.
9. Quoted in Igou, *The Amish in Their Own Words*, p. 243.
10. Quoted in Igou, *The Amish in Their Own Words*, p. 235.
11. Wayne Weaver, *Dust Between My Toes: An Amish Boy's Journey*. Wooster, OH: Wooster Book Company, 1997, p. 23.
12. Bender, *Plain and Simple*, p. 37.
13. Kraybill, *The Riddle of Amish Culture*, p. 52.
14. Quoted in Igou, *The Amish in Their Own Words*, p. 57.
15. Quoted in Sara E. Fisher and Rachel K. Stahl, *The Amish School*. Intercourse, PA: Good Books, 1997, p. 62.
16. Kraybill, *The Riddle of Amish Culture*, p. 60.
17. Bender, *Plain and Simple*, p. 59.
18. Quoted in Igou, *The Amish in Their Own Words*, p. 61.
19. Quoted in Hostetler, *Amish Society*, p. 368.

Chapter 2: A Community of Believers

20. Quoted in Igou, *The Amish in Their Own Words*, p. 26.
21. Quoted in Hostetler, *Amish Society*, p. 47.
22. Quoted in Hostetler, *Amish Society*, p. 62.
23. Quoted in Hostetler, *Amish Society*, p. 56.
24. Steven M. Nolt, *A History of the Amish*. Intercourse, PA: Good Books, 1992, p. 63.
25. Quoted in Igou, *The Amish in Their Own Words*, p. 120.
26. Quoted in Chris Newton, "Neighbors Worry Whether Families Can Survive Texas Weather Without Modern Conveniences," *Dallas Morning News*, June 7, 1998, p. 35A.
27. Quoted in Newton, "Neighbors Worry Whether Families Can Survive Texas," p. 35A.
28. Quoted in Newton, "Neighbors Worry Whether Families Can Survive Texas," p. 35A.
29. Quoted in "Amish Say Adieu to Tazewell County," *Washington Times*, March 15, 1999, p. C6.
30. Quoted in Bender, *Plain and Simple*, p. 68.
31. Quoted in Igou, *The Amish in Their Own Words*, p. 205.
32. Quoted in Hostetler, *Amish Society*, p. 86.
33. Weaver, *Dust Between My Toes*, p. 28.
34. Eric Brende, "Harvest on Gideon's Farm," *Mother Earth News*, December 10, 1996, p. 14(4).

35. Quoted in Hostetler, *Amish Society*, p. 227.

Chapter 3: Patterns of Worship

36. Hostetler, *Amish Society*, p. 210.
37. Hostetler, *Amish Society*, p. 210.
38. Hostetler, *Amish Society*, p. 210.
39. Quoted in Igou, *The Amish in Their Own Words*, p. 179.
40. Quoted in Igou, *The Amish in Their Own Words*, p. 187.
41. Quoted in Bender, *Plain and Simple*, p. 68.
42. Bender, *Plain and Simple*, p. 68.
43. Hostetler, *Amish Society*, p. 82.
44. Quoted in Igou, *The Amish in Their Own Words*, p. 188.
45. Quoted in Kraybill, *The Riddle of Amish Culture*, p. 108.
46. Quoted in Igou, *The Amish in Their Own Words*, p. 192.
47. Hostetler, *Amish Society*, p. 225.
48. Hostetler, *Amish Society*, p. 148.
49. Jim Butterfield, *Driving the Amish*. Scottdale, PA: Herald Press, 1997, p. 29.
50. Quoted in Igou, *The Amish in Their Own Words*, p. 286.
51. Quoted in Butterfield, *Driving the Amish*, p. 104.

Chapter 4: A Time for Everything

52. Quoted in Igou, *The Amish in Their Own Words*, p. 142.
53. Quoted in Igou, *The Amish in Their Own Words*, p. 111.
54. Kraybill, *The Riddle of Amish Culture*, p. 39.
55. Weaver, *Dust Between My Toes*, p. 19.
56. Quoted in Igou, *The Amish in Their Own Words*, pp. 99–100.
57. Butterfield, *Driving the Amish*, p. 17.
58. Stephen Scott and Kenneth Pellman, *Living Without Electricity*. Intercourse, PA: Good Books, 1990, p.17.

59. Scott and Pellman, *Living Without Electricity*, p. 25.
60. Bender, *Plain and Simple*, p. 76.
61. Martha Moore Davis, *Sarah's Seasons: An Amish Diary and Conversation*. Iowa City: University of Iowa Press, 1997, p. 49.
62. Quoted in George M. Kreps, Joseph F. Donnermeyer, and Marty W. Kreps, *A Quiet Moment in Time: A Contemporary View of Amish Society*. Walnut Creek, OH: Carlisle Press, 1997, pp. 78–79.
63. Butterfield, *Driving the Amish*, p. 79.
64. Quoted in Igou, *The Amish in Their Own Words*, p. 83.
65. Bender, *Plain and Simple*, p. 59.
66. Bender, *Plain and Simple*, p. 95.
67. Bender, *Plain and Simple*, p. 48.
68. Weaver, *Dust Between My Toes*, p. 34.
69. Quoted in Igou, *The Amish in Their Own Words*, p. 147.

Chapter 5: Our Own Schools

70. Louise Stoltzfus, *Amish Women*. Intercourse, PA: Good Books, 1994, p. 31.
71. Hostetler, *Amish Society*, p. 179.
72. Hostetler, *Amish Society*, p. 179.
73. Quoted in Butterfield, *Driving the Amish*, p. 80.
74. Quoted in Igou, *The Amish in Their Own Words*, p. 143.
75. Quoted in Kraybill, *The Riddle of Amish Culture*, p. 121.
76. Fisher and Stahl, *The Amish School*, p. 9.
77. Quoted in Fisher and Stahl, *The Amish School*, p. 7.
78. Quoted in Fisher and Stahl, *The Amish School*, p. 9.
79. Fisher and Stahl, *The Amish School*, p. 88.
80. Quoted in Kraybill, *The Riddle of Amish Culture*, p. 121.
81. Butterfield, *Driving the Amish*, p. 77.

82. Quoted in Fisher and Stahl, *The Amish School*, p. 31.

83. Stoltzfus, *Amish Women*, p. 32.

84. Quoted in Fisher and Stahl, *The Amish School*, p. 53.

85. Quoted in Butterfield, *Driving the Amish*, p. 79.

86. Quoted in Fisher and Stahl, *The Amish School*, p. 48.

87. Quoted in Butterfield, *Driving the Amish*, p. 75.

88. Quoted in Fisher and Stahl, *The Amish School*, p. 48.

89. Quoted in Fisher and Stahl, *The Amish School*, p. 82.

90. Fisher and Stahl, *The Amish School*, p. 4.

Chapter 6: Interaction with *Englishers*

91. Quoted in Igou, *The Amish in Their Own Words*, p. 336.

92. Quoted in Sean Gorman, "House Passes Measure to Allow Younger Amish Woodworkers," States News Service, March 4, 1999.

93. Quoted in Gorman, "House Passes Measure to Allow Younger Amish Woodworkers."

94. "Drug Problems of the Amish Brought to Light by 2 Arrests: Community Concerned with Public Perception of Usually Reclusive Members," *Dallas Morning News*, June 28, 1998, p. 10A.

95. Quoted in "Amish Teens' Drinking Upsets Iowa Community: Flirtations with Worldly Ways Leads Them to Legal Trouble," *Dallas Morning News*, June 19, 1999, p. 5A.

96. Quoted in "Amish Aim to Curb Underage Drinking," Associated Press, May 29, 2000.

97. Quoted in "Amish in State Suffer Vandalism—Police Upset They 'Turned Other Cheek,'" *Capital Times* (Madison, WI), November 8, 1997, p. 1A.

98. Quoted in Jamie Talan, "Research Among the Amish," *Newsday*, May 28, 1996, p. B29.

99. Quoted in Igou, *The Amish in Their Own Words*, p. 304.

100. Quoted in Igou, *The Amish in Their Own Words*, p. 303.

101. Quoted in Jim Landers, "Sprawl Changing Amish Country: Pennsylvania County Grapples with Growth Plan," *Dallas Morning News*, October 5, 1999, p. 1A.

102. Quoted in Igou, *The Amish in Their Own Words*, p. 306.

103. Quoted in Hostetler, *Amish Society*, p. 319.

104. Quoted in Jennifer Brown, "Old Order Amish Plainly Flourishing: Growing Group Goes Against the Grain in Century of Technology," *Washington Times*, October 18, 1999, p. C4.

105. Quoted in Mike Harden, "More Amish Leave Farms to Build Businesses," *Minneapolis Star Tribune*, January 2, 1996, p. 3E.

106. Harden, "More Amish Leave Farms to Build Businesses," p. 3E.

107. Tom Ragan, "Amish Are Leaving the Farms and Opening Up Businesses," AP Online, March 9, 1998.

108. Quoted in Carleen Hawn, "A Second Parting of the Red Sea," *Forbes*, March 9, 1998.

109. Quoted in Donald B. Kraybill and Marc A. Olshan, eds., *The Amish Struggle with Modernity*. Hanover and London: University Press of New England, 1994, p. 172.

110. Donald B. Kraybill and Marc A. Olshan, *The Amish Struggle with Modernity*, p. 172.

111. Quoted in Igou, *The Amish in Their Own Words*, p. 134.

112. Quoted in Igou, *The Amish in Their Own Words*, p. 66.

For Further Reading

Richard Ammon, *Growing Up Amish*. New York: Atheneum, 1989. Ammon describes the day-to-day life of a typical Amish child. The book includes photos, common myths about the Amish, songs, poems, and recipes.

Raymond Bial, *Amish Home*. Boston: Houghton Mifflin, 1993. Beautiful photographs and accompanying text show a typical Amish home.

Doris Faber, *The Amish*. Illustrated by Michael E. Erkel. New York: Doubleday, 1991. An easy-to-read, illustrated book summarizing Amish life.

Merle Good and Phyllis Good, *20 Most Asked Questions About the Amish and Mennon-ites*. Intercourse, PA: Good Books, 1995. Answers the most frequently asked questions about these two Anabaptist sects.

Phyllis Pellman Good, Kate Good, and Rebecca Good, *Amish Cooking for Kids: For 6-to-12-Year-Old Cooks*. Intercourse, PA: Good Books, 1999. Offers step-by-step directions for making Amish recipes ranging from Whoopie Pies to Bread Soup.

David Kline, *Great Possessions: An Amish Farmer's Journal*. Berkeley, CA: North Point Press, 1990. A series of essays on nature, farming, and animals by an Amish farmer.

Works Consulted

Books

Sue Bender, *Plain and Simple: A Woman's Journey to the Amish*. New York: HarperCollins, 1989. An artist's chronicle of self-discovery after an extended stay with the Amish.

Jim Butterfield, *Driving the Amish*. Scottdale, PA: Herald Press, 1997. Butterfield, a retired bus driver, tells about his experiences driving the Amish in rural Ohio. Includes stunning photographs by Doyle Yoder.

Martha Moore Davis, *Sarah's Seasons: An Amish Diary and Conversation*. Iowa City: University of Iowa Press, 1997. Contains the journal entries of Sarah Fisher, an Amish wife and mother.

Sara E. Fisher and Rachel K. Stahl, *The Amish School*. Intercourse, PA: Good Books, 1997. This collection of solid information about the Amish school system includes excerpts from the diary of an Amish schoolgirl.

John A. Hostetler, *Amish Roots: A Treasury of History, Wisdom, and Lore*. Baltimore: Johns Hopkins University Press, 1989. A collection of letters, journal entries, poems, and stories by the Amish. Topics include schools and school management, home and family, misfortunes, and legends.

———, *Amish Society*. 4th ed. Baltimore: Johns Hopkins University Press, 1993. This definitive study covers nearly all aspects of Amish life.

Brad Igou, comp., *The Amish in Their Own Words: Amish Writings from 25 Years of* Family Life *Magazine*. Scottdale, PA: Herald Press, 1999. A collection of excerpts from *Family Life*, an Amish magazine. Topics covered include controversies, marriage, and farm work.

Grace H. Kaiser, *Detour*. Intercourse, PA: Good Books, 1990. Memoir by a woman doctor who served the Amish for nearly thirty years.

David Kline, *Scratching the Woodchuck: Nature on an Amish Farm*. Athens: University of Georgia Press, 1997. More essays by an Amish farmer about the simple pleasures of nature.

Donald B. Kraybill, *The Riddle of Amish Culture*. Baltimore: Johns Hopkins University Press, 1991. A sociologist attempts to explain some of the more puzzling aspects of Amish life.

Donald B. Kraybill and Marc A. Olshan, eds., *The Amish Struggle with Modernity*. Hanover and London: University Press of New England, 1994. Includes essays on social and occupational changes within the Amish community.

George M. Kreps, Joseph F. Donnermeyer, and Marty W. Kreps, *A Quiet Moment in Time: A Contemporary View of Amish Society*. Walnut Creek, OH: Carlisle Press, 1997. Provides an easy-to-understand overview of the Amish. Also gives tips on how to get the most out of a visit to an Amish community.

Kathleen McLary, *Amish Style: Clothing, Home Furnishing, Toys, Dolls, and Quilts*. Bloomington and Indianapolis: Indiana University Press, 1993. Simple, easy-to-read text and detailed, colored photographs of Amish items.

Steven M. Nolt, *A History of the Amish*. Intercourse, PA: Good Books, 1992. Presents the struggles of the Amish from their beginnings to the early 1990s.

Patrick Quillin, *Amish Folk Medicine*. North Canton, OH: The Leader Co., Inc., 1995. Lists home remedies Amish people turn to cure health problems ranging from backaches to sore throats.

Stephen Scott, *The Amish Wedding*. Intercourse, PA: Good Books, 1988. Provides information on weddings, baptisms, Sunday services, funerals, and other special days of Old Order groups.

———, *Plain Buggies: Amish, Mennonite, and Brethren Horse-Drawn Transportation*. Intercourse, PA: Good Books, 1981. Learn about the various types of buggies that Old Order groups use.

———, *Why Do They Dress That Way?* Intercourse, PA: Good Books, 1986. A detailed look at the clothing of the plain people.

Stephen Scott and Kenneth Pellman, *Living Without Electricity*. Intercourse, PA: Good Books, 1990. Offers clear explanations on how the Amish use alternative sources of power instead of electricity.

Louise Stoltzfus, *Amish Women*. Intercourse, PA: Good Books, 1994. The author, who grew up Amish, profiles ten Amish women, showing how they have found a place for themselves within the bounds of their tightly knit, strict community.

Wayne Weaver, *Dust Between My Toes: An Amish Boy's Journey*. Wooster, OH: Wooster Book Company, 1997. A physician who was reared in the Amish religion tells what it was like growing up in rural Ohio and how he became a doctor.

Periodicals

"Amish Aim to Curb Underage Drinking," Associated Press, May 29, 2000.

"Amish Children Encouraged to Play Games in the Name of Safety," *Dallas Morning News*, July 1, 2000.

"Amish in State Suffer Vandalism—Police Upset They 'Turned Other Cheek,'" *Capital Times* (Madison, WI), November 8, 1997.

"Amish Say Adieu to Tazewell County," *Washington Times*, March 15, 1999.

"Amish Teens' Drinking Upsets Iowa Community: Flirtations with Worldly Ways Leads Them to Legal Trouble," *Dallas Morning News*, June 19, 1999.

Eric Brende, "Harvest on Gideon's Farm," *Mother Earth News*, December 10, 1996.

Jennifer Brown, "Old Order Amish Plainly Flourishing: Growing Group Goes Against the Grain in Century of Technology," *Washington Times*, October 18, 1999.

"Drug Problems of the Amish Brought to Light by 2 Arrests: Community Concerned with Public Perception of Usually Reclusive Members," *Dallas Morning News*, June 28, 1998.

Sean Gorman, "House Passes Measure to Allow Younger Amish Woodworkers," States News Service, March 4, 1999.

Mike Harden, "More Amish Leave Farms to Build Businesses," *Minneapolis Star Tribune*, January 2, 1996.

Carleen Hawn, "A Second Parting of the Red Sea," *Forbes*, March 9, 1998.

Katy Kelly, "'Doc Lehman' is a Bridge to Divergent Worlds," *USA Today*, June 9, 1998.

Jim Landers, "Sprawl Changing Amish Country: Pennsylvania County Grapples with Growth Plan," *Dallas Morning News*, October 5, 1999.

Jeanne Marie Laskas, "Fire, Hope, and Charity: A Secluded Amish Valley Emerges from a Night of Chaos and Terror into a Daylight of Love and Renewal," *Life*, June 1, 1992.

Phil McDade, "A Quilting People—Annual Amish Auction Attracts Crafts of All Kinds," *Wisconsin State Journal*, August 4, 1997.

Chris Newton, "Neighbors Worry Whether Families Can Survive Texas Weather Without Modern Conveniences," *Dallas Morning News*, June 7, 1998.

Tom Ragan, "Amish Are Leaving the Farms and Opening Up Businesses," AP Online, March 9, 1998.

Amy Sancetta, "Taking Books to TV-free Territory: Ohio County's Library on Wheels Seeds Amish Children," *Washington Times*, August 20, 2000.

Jamie Talan, "Research Among the Amish," *Newsday*, May 28, 1996.

Index

Picture Credits

About the Author

Although she now calls Chicago, Illinois, home, Katherine Wagner previously lived in Florida, Michigan, Ohio, Oregon, Utah, and Washington State. After receiving a degree in business, she landed a position as business manager for an internationally acclaimed dance troupe. Later, she worked as a general assignment reporter and has been a correspondent for several daily newspapers. Wagner writes for a variety of magazines, online publications, and children's textbook publishers. In her free time, she enjoys feeding wild birds, participating in recreational sports, and studying American Sign Language (ASL).